POEMS AND SHORT STORIES

OF SEYCHELLES AND BEYOND

By

Marion Zarqani Gendron

PANGAEA PORTRAITS

Published in 2013
Poems and Short Stories of Seychelles and Beyond
Marion Zarqani Gendron

Published by Pangaea Portraits Ltd, PO Box 336, Maritime House, Victoria, Seychelles. Email: pangaea@sky.com

ISBN: 978-1-291-62057-3

TO:

RIEUL AND TYRIAN

For being such loving and wonderful sons!

ACKNOWLEDGEMENTS

Thank you Adrian Skerrett for all your assistance with the publication and Rieul for the finishing touches.

CONTENTS

FOREWORD

Many famous people have attempted to define poetry as "the spontaneous overflow of powerful feelings" (Wordsworth) or "what makes one laugh or cry or yawn" (Dylan Thomas).

I have written a few poems and narratives because of a compelling and natural urge to share some thought and feeling with others, in a form and shape that I hope can best convey them. Words are creative tools that can be wielded to evoke a sentiment or provoke a thought or idea, deeply embedded in our consciousness. These moments are often triggered by an event, an encounter or an experience; mundane or dramatic–that can hold a world of meaning.

All the stories are real life experiences. Many are about holiday travel within the Seychelles granitic islands and they attempt to convey the nostalgic beauty of a fast changing environment.

Some of the themes that weave their way in the following pages are: the tragedy of war, poverty, death, gender issues, social disintegration, faith and the impact of economic development on the beauty of our natural landscapes.

The Writings of the Bahá'í Faith have been a source of inspiration and it is a message of hope for a new world order, emerging out of the current gloom and turmoil that surrounds us.

THE CALL

The silent mounds so gently call,
through the icy walls
and burrow warmth
of inner sanctuary.

As embers fade over frosty earth,
the mystical bells will lure you on,
to dry the tears of choices made
in nature's womb.

A new-born day dispels the flicker
in awesome splendour,
then fades away on a dying mist,
in a wistful moment of ritual delight.

1983

FORMER DAYS

Swollen streams and straying
strands.
Endless plains of distant
strains.
Sacred lakes on beds
of brass.
Crimson waves in purple
haze,
weaving shades in spiral
maze.
Restless flares on frosted
ferns.
Rearing domes in daunting
robes.
Silken threads and silent
thrones.
Hidden stones from forest
troves.
Fluttering flags
on mountain crags,
as empty shells the echoes
end.

1986

VISIT TO THE CEMETERY

A diminishing mound
in the vanishing light.
A crumpled heap
of withering bloom.
Stark reflections
are pallid against
a cloudless luminosity
that slowly imbues
the hollow core of my existence.

Warmth envelops
a universe of minds
as all my achievements
in a single rose
I lay at your feet,

my dearest.

1995

SCARS

In Siliguri lanes, they await the rains.
The wheels they turn, inexorably drawn.

The reins relinquished,
all light's extinguished.

Then giant orbs slowly drift
into nature's merciful gift,
as voices creep down corridors of sleep
in a distant whirlwind
of grey, starched uniforms.

Scarlet testimony, silent wails
of winter days and mountain ways,

and hope that lay in eyes so deep,
rests at the curling toes of blissful sleep,

floating through the night
in seas of burning light.

Amidst the dancing rocks and unlit tapestries,
they scaled the heights of unravelled mysteries,
and the earth now heaves in even monotone,
as ripples fade over seas intoned,
that imbibe the silt of the eroded shores,
to mirror the vision
of the coral sands.

1986

THE RICKSHAW

A coppery wraith
in faded shades;
a vanishing dream,
in the twilight haze
of an eternal cycle.

In the gripping wake
of gravity's pull,
he mirrors the glaze
of a finite horizon
at the crest of a hill.

They leave behind
the marble fountains
and cascades of red velvet
that topples into
the liberated multitudes.

As inches he scores,
his strength
ebbs away,
in an infinitesimal heap
of loose change.

At the far rear,
propped in plump hands,
stifling the belch

of an indulgent afternoon,
rests a bulging briefcase.

They inspect with disdain
the urchin's handiwork,
to sink with resignation
in the sheltered alcove
of a lifetime's debt.

Above the giant wings
that roar in the sunrise,
her glistening eyes
close on the knowledge
of a disappearing fatherland.

1986

LISTEN

Listen to the voice of youth... listen...

stepping on stones in mighty torrents,
twining ropes of forest lianas,
poking at crispy, curled up leaves.

Listen to the voice of youth...listen...

trailing cowbells in greenest pastures,
carving footsteps in virgin snow,
swaying by firelight on frosty nights.

Listen to the voice of youth... listen...

hurtling at windmills with redoubtable fervour,
completing a journey that never began,
questing for answers that lie in the question.

Listen to the voice of youth... listen...

mapping the future on ink-covered paper,
feathering objectives with the vast unreality
of conceiving plans on the path of action.

Listen to the voice of youth... listen...

walking the empty corridors of power,

high...on a precarious tightrope,
dangling over mountains of shredded paper.

Listen to the voice of youth... listen...
trapped in the kernel of your adolescence,

then...
crash in waves of endless pain,
churn in a mass of foaming froth,
grind to a film of silken sand,

and float...
in the salt-laden
mists of time.

1999

A HOT BATH

Fluid warmth
of softest form,
as spirals melt
the crystal shine
of purest light,
with glows that break
the bounds that bind
the sleeping tide
in earth's dark mind,
and stretches far
to touch the heights
of deepest flight.

1994

THE RITUAL

He rises from wood smoke screens,
weaving an evanescent spiral,

in the receding firelight,
under a flickering starlight.

Then the drums summon;
the cymbals call.

He oscillates to the rhythm
of the tide,

sways to the melody of the palms
thrilling to the call of the wild,

still the drums summon;
the cymbals call.

He jerks to the beat of the quivering hides,
pulses to the twang of the distant strings,

drenched in the turgid heat
of the tropical night,

still the drums summon;
the cymbals call.

Then the dawn breaks the shadows!

Clicking heels on hardest asphalt
and coolest chignon perched high aloft

over mincing words on brittle glasses,
draws the blinds over landscapes old,

to cherish less
the images of firelight.

1990

THE POWER OF LOVE

Worlds collide
in swirling dust
and clouds of starburst,
as Andromeda lights
the pathway home.

Clusters ignite
to fade and flare
in the flux of time,
and circle Orion
with the heat of youth
in a game of chance.

A universe expands
into empty space,
capturing spheres
where Cepheids roam.

Constellations merge
and galaxies form
from relative weight.

But the greatest force
that shaped the atoms
of a forgotten Eden
into structure and form,
is the power of Love.

1998.

THE PAIR

Their rainbow hues span the heavens
when weathers fuse.

At the name of spades, into limitless space
the centre fades.

The sight once seen, in unknown ways
they hurry unseen.

They touch the surface in the calmness of knowledge
to arrest the pace.

Far out in the woods, the leaves that fall
suit autumn moods.

The paths once strewn beneath serene skies
are never green.

And now they call
with silent voices
in empty halls,
and music will play
to fill the void
till the call of day.

1994

GOAL

He clutched his hope all too close,
and victory's post–
a necrose blur of scarlet and white,
flashes past the hooded cars on country lanes.

The fervid touch of summer noon
and rabid cries on pounding turf,
unleash the might of grimmer days
and straining sinews of Calliope the muse.

Those guns or missiles faced no retreat,
and ghosts will answer to that single call;
a likeness remote to that unblinking stare,
gazing far beyond
the spruced grey uniform and crystal chandeliers,
to a lonely podium in a whitewashed alley.

The ad misericordiam of a silenced crowd
echoes from a tormented past
to a glorious dawn.
Seychelles hails you!
Columbia's sons and daughters
know of battles won
that you just lost,
at the count of six.

1994

BAIE LAZARE

The words we utter
are lost in forest gloom,
that deepens around
the little brick house,
where the means
once stretched
and work suspended,
she lies trapped –
in the final ignominy
of domestic triviality.

And the morning sun
casts her shadows
and sheds no warmth
on that solitary bay,
where the battling limbs
gave up the fight,
to free a mind
that dared to choose.

1996

SIXTY

He wept the tears of a bygone age
and held the dream of whispering palms.

He heaved the sighs of laden thatch
and stiffened resolve in forlorn folk.

He wandered barefoot on distant sands
but fixed his gaze on beckoning skies.

He raised aloft those triple colours,
that spoke of philosophy's shame and glory.

He scattered the strains of humble merriment
across the seas and furthest continents.

Now the battle rages between friend and foe
about the means and the ends,
but some just crouch in prayerful poise,
at the threshold of the vision beyond.

Like the gems that shone from that darkest continent,
the riches they sought lay deep within.
But between the glass and the crystal
shines the light of purest motive,
alone acceptable unto Him.

1995

DROUGHT

We wait for the rains,
but all in vain.

The oceans cool
as systems eastward lie.
Dwindling streams trickle into shrunken ponds,
where weeds do sprout from crackling beds.
Leaden pipes belching air from tight-closed valves,
as we that walk in dust clouds
seldom blink.

Then speculations mount
as the waterline dips to its lowest ebb,
that spectres rise from open case files,
in the mud and slime
the years piled up in their hidden depths.

We yearn for the rains
for economic gains.

But the bats at dusk
screech over marshy land.
In the open fields,
the mountain streams
are devoid of strains of latter days.

In the crowded spaces,

the filth now flows
from gutters and sewers
to kitchen and sink –
right down to the fingertips.
But the grime won't wash
till evening descends
to wipe the traces away.

Still we quaff of some rusty dregs
that shrinks the bowels
and wrench soft tissue in baneful ways,
to swallow the pills of many colours
from uniformed men
across polished counters.

Then the clouds smother the brilliance of the moon.
A lone star twinkles in the mid-most heaven.

We lift our faces to the great downpour,
run with the wind that lifts our sails,
dance to the rhythm of the falling leaves,
drench the heat that melts away
the rainbow hues of devils' unions,
wildest blossoms strew on stony ground,
and cast ourselves in nature's arms
to reap the fruits of honest toil.

1998

THE SCHOOLGIRL

Undulating desert dunes
and warm ocean currents.
Caves of crystal white
and frontiers carved
in hills of precious ore.
Windswept plains
that fills with golden corn
and mountain streams
of melting snow.

The images spark
behind bulging eyeballs,
a haunting nightmare
between softest thighs
just out of diapers.

And the persistent ring
that brings relief to teenage hearts
only fills with dread,
for she sees not beyond
the glint of a blade in a deserted alley
beneath gleaming walls
of purchased privacy,
and the stunted growth of a childhood
that...
will never blossom.

1996

LUCRETIA LOVE

Across oceans of desire,
music of sound
and stars that dance
amidst golden curls and velvet furs
on cherished billboards
of antiquity framed.

A simple wreath of white spring blossom
in the depths of silence
and a last bow –
before the rape set in.

Then the wheels skid into empty space
and the world was too small
till you reigned again,
in a little tin shack amidst all your artefacts
and cast long shadows
as beauty dipped behind tropical shades.

I'll take your hand
Lucretia Love,
and on that precipitous slope
with the chorus at dawn,
together await
the final outcome.

1996.

FIRE

When sirens blared,
silence seized the thoughtless mind
in endless sighs...

Voices pitched in pure despair
drew no more than a casual shrug,
as we refuge sought in a set routine.

The weeds she tossed in amorphous heaps,
sprouted once in the momentary sunshine
thirsting for the morning dew,

then the empires of the biblical sons–
a mere handful of dust
in a house of ashes.

He rises now from ocean depths
and forest glades,
luring her to empty space,

flaps his wings on bended knees,
crouching in deepest shades
where whispers never fade;

"Manman, pa kit boy tou sel!"
(mummy, don't leave me alone)

1996.

BAHÁ'U'LLÁH

Hope shone through her radiant being,
as torrents descended
in slumbering moments.

She raised her hands.
The heavens opened!
The trumpets sounded thrice!

But He was cast to the winds and snow
of the harshest winters
and the galling chains of fifty and more.

He watered the desert with all the agony
of Adam's descent, as the red roan stallion
ploughed the clouds in the mists of morn.

Across the shore less ocean, the little fishes clung
to every filament of the sacred locks,
to swim in the circles of purest light.

He melted the will of the agents of death
with the soul-piercing gaze
from the shores of the Caspian,

and those who inhaled
the fragrance of the rose
bled on the thorns of the Crimson hill.

The peals of derision from palace walls,
echoed the crash of the mightiest empires,
and the footsteps of the white-haired Prisoner.

Now Carmel is decked in green and gold,
for the scion of Jesse has come home at last,
to a throne of unrivalled glory

and His Ark will sail the seas of fulfilment,
five thousand centuries,
in the dawning of the Age.

1996.

BELOVED

In the euphony of dawn,
the light shines in letters of gold.
As the bow ploughs the cerulean waters,
an emblazoned horizon
matches the zeal of tempestuous youth.

You etched His Glory on effaceless shores,
to chisel it anew on loftiest summits
and give new birth
amidst the stars that shine
in the far recesses of an unfolding might.

The pernicious blows
on that resilient bark of a myriad hues,
first drew the sap of its inmost being,
and then were bathed in the eutrophic waters
of a pervading love.

The heavy steps receded from
the committee rooms and action-packed halls
as the relentless surf of your beloved isle
cast you on the alien shores
of temporary retreat.

Your implorations touched
that hallowed spot,
and the fiery herald spent its feathers

those sixty new morns,
to burst its cage on the brilliance
of its vitreous image.

The infant still throbs
in those precious moments
of childhood motion,
as fingertips press a thousand drops
of crystal fragrance,
to chase the chill
of desperate longing.

In the deepest nights,
the wings that labour to shelter us
from rain and wind,
entrammelled and spent,
quivered and soared
in profulgence of joy,
at the silent call of your true Beloved.

Your roots now yield
the efflorescence of knowledge,
whose branches will feed
in a soil well charged
with the ions of vitality,
to cast its seeds
in the pristine enclaves
of boundless freedom.

1995

THREE LITTLE FISHES

She sat all alone
on the city sidewalk,
just a little forlorn,
away from the shore.

She cooks all alone
where the main artery
pulsates toxic fumes
into shuttered minds,

She stays well engrossed
beside skidding wheels
and wisps of smoke
from smouldering rot.

Plucked from the street
and the choicest menu,
the *bombils* are placed
on well trodden paths.

How many mouths they'll feed;
how many meals they'll stretch,
I'll forever wonder
as she fades away
in the land of the two *'mussouns'*

1999

THE RETURN

A distant call
precedes the fall.

The roots are deep
that patience reaps.

You turn the tide
with faintest sign.

We seize the night
with arms of might

to feed the flock
with hearts that rock

and make of light
just a neon sight.

We find the stars
and travel far,

for touch is soft
of minds aloft.

We fill the sheets
with shades of bliss

and ride the flood
on wings of doves.

You etch the lines
all cause defies.

We hold the clock
for ships that dock

and scale the peak
but never seek

to plunge ahead
and find instead

what lies ahead
is but a guess,

and hope evokes
a rope that chokes.

1999

TAHIRIH

She ripped the veils of countless centuries
as her beauty shone for the world to see,

in a little hamlet,
in the land of Kha.

Freed from the shackles of a tyrant's love,
from the curtains stepped
a prodigy of her time,
first woman apostle,
a clergyman's daughter,
and heroine of a thousand eulogies,

They rushed to and fro
in shock and in grief
at 'modesty' foregone–
to the castles fleeing
and mountain retreats–
swords unsheathing,
life blood spilling,
even faith relinquishing,

in a little hamlet,
in the land of Kha.

She embraced the life
of a hunted fugitive

with lyrical joy
and lived the vision
of a heron's flight
at the break of day
to free the oppressed
of the opposite sex
from east to the west,
casting aside
all kingly offers
of fame and fortune.

Then morning broke!
Soldiers came knocking.
In a long bridal gown of purest white silk
and string of white pearls
they found her waiting...praying.

In an abandoned well outside the city gates
under a heap of rubble,
they saw her cast,
her silken handkerchief round her slender throat.

They carried her tenderly into the minds and hearts
that will not break or bend under tyranny's will,
till the gales of change fan the sparks of equality,
that devour the crumbing edifices
to build everything anew.

1999

THE THREE ONENESSES

God is one–
the *om tat sat*
of human existence.
Why split the sun
from rays on high,
reflections' might
in mirrors of light;
forge mortal bonds
from spiritual songs?

Religions are one
when all is done–
born of the essence
of Love and Truth.
Why chapters rip
from a single book?
The lamp love more
than the light it bore?

So Belfast wails
but digs in her spurs.
Afghan caves spew forth
demented spawn,
while dirgeful streams
of vanquished dreams
cross steel frontiers
from Balkan graves
to Gaza camps,

from maimed Africa
to flames of East Timor,
the seeds of death
planted deep
in the spoils of war.

The earth's one country,
mankind its citizens.
Why hack at heads
of rearing intolerance
with knives of partition
and build up walls
that must come down?

The diamond fields lie
behind barbed wire fences,
and oil fields still pump
a regulated supply
of luxury and ease,
while the desert steals
from hungry mouths
and dumpers roll by ocean shores
to combat evils
of market fluctuations.

Sing the three onenesses,
O steeple and mosque!
March with the beat
of the song of the wind
Family, tribe, nation arise!
Your age of maturity's here.

1999

JOURNEY

In the valley of Search,
on the steed of patience,
every Jacob yearns
for his beloved Joseph.
Tears rain down
as the longing hearts
even dust heaps sift
for a single trace
of the Invisible One.

In the valley of Love,
on the steed of suffering,
enter the desert of Egypt,
where poison tastes like honey.
Past the vale of shadows,
the leviathan of love
swallows the master of reason
and the wisdom of the sages.

In the valley of Knowledge,
the ocean is in a drop,
the sun in an atom.
Find peace in war,
friendship in anger,
for light has shattered
the nights of longing.

In the valley of Unity,
devoid of rank or title,
beyond veils of plurality,
a dream can hold
a thousand secrets.
Every object mirrors
the light of the sun
in myriad colours.

In the valley of true Felicity,
the throne of glory
sits upon the dust.
In the silence of wisdom,
reality in illusion
is the source of re-creation.

In the valley of Wonderment,
true wealth lies in poverty,
liberty in humility.
You travel without moving,
speak without a tongue.
The universe lies within.

In the valley of true Poverty
and absolute nothingness,
every branch will not flower,
all oceans yield not pearls.
The man of vision
gives up the drop of life
to swim in mystic waters,
finds a mystery in every letter

sees the world in every city,
hears a song in every prairie.

But dogs will chase
the gazelle of the desert,
and pitiless crows
 the bird in flight.
Jealous hunters track
the maiden of the prairie
and the faithful heart drowns
in rivers of blood.

Seven steps, O traveller,
even as seven breaths!
Seven valleys lie
on your journey home.

2000

Based on "The Seven Valleys"
by Bahá'u'lláh

INSPIRATION

True inspiration,
is a mighty torrent
from the highest peak,
in an earthly guise
robbed of human will,
like a stainless leaf
from the tallest tree
just blown about
by relentless winds.

True inspiration,
are Words divine
on pages bound,
like choicest wine
in cellars fine
or pearls that shine
in ocean mines.

True inspiration
is pain and sorrow,
beauty and joy
in perfect harmony–
the melody of truth
that soars to heaven
from simple chords;
the philosophy of eternity,
and sweetness of forgiveness.

True inspiration
is the breeze that wafts
in the mystical dawn
over slumbering souls–
the magic of mystery
 that casts its spell
on discerning ones,
weaving a tapestry of brilliant colours
for the lonely wayfarer.

True inspiration is the crimson stains
beneath the dust–
a furrowed brow,
riddled with scars
like crusaders walls,
but softened by smiles
of utter contentment
that kindles the heart
for a thousand miles.

True inspiration is the dew
that awakens the morning blossom,
a spark that ignites an undying flame,
a transcendental tide,
that ebbs and flows
on the shores
of the inner vision.

2000

THE PHOTOGRAPH

I see,
oceans of tribulations,
that all the crimson seas
if turned to ink,
are powerless to record.

I see,
the anguish of a thousand betrayals,
a generation
that only proffered
the cup of its own venom.

I see,
the ordeals of bygone ages
surpassed,
a Gethsemane of forty years
locked in an impenetrable gaze.

I see,
a countenance framed by long black locks,
its freshness dimmed,
as agonies rain down
from the clouds above and the earth below.

I hear,
the scourge of the bastinado,

chains so heavy,
lacerations so deep,
as to bow the noblest head
that ever walked the surface of the earth.

I hear,
a body stoned by a fanatical mob,
deprived of warmth,
even bread and water;
no place to lay down
His weary head.

I see,
a wraith-like form
wasted and worn,
light as a breath,
that the billowing robes cannot hide
and I bow my head in shame
at what human hands
have wrought
and vow to dedicate
my remaining years
to the remembrance of His.

Haifa, 2001

THE THRESHOLD

Natural light filters down
to the verdant isle below,
in memory of nature's greatest Love.
There she kneels to exhaust
her long, long list of prayers
each with objectives specific;
well planned and perfectly executed.

A few steps more
to the sacred threshold,
where circle the celestial concourse
and candles weep their lives away,
while bright red blossoms
are forever fragrant and warm
in the midnight stillness
and softest white petals
cling to anguished brows.

Her dark head sinks to the earth's bosom
in an agonizing farewell
to the heavenly days of sweet reunion
when suddenly, the heavens open!

A majestic form,
bearing the twin features
of the Herald and Glory,
enthroned and still…

plunges earthwards
in a cosmic cataclysm–
a power and force so intense,
that a billion bolts of lightning
are a mere shimmer.
All matter's reduced to non-existence.
She has no form or substance.
There is no time or space.

The cascading, swirling light is
too piercing to behold,
veiling a presence
into Whose vortex
the entire universe,
less than a grain of dust, catapults.

It is the meaning and the purpose!
It is the truth and the essence!
It is the past and the present!
It feels like the beginning and the end!

She is lifted to a plane
of unimaginable dimensions,
of awesome certainty,
and absolute wonderment.

In a moment so brief,
engraved from the realms on high,
in the silent, penetrating voice of letters,
was the compelling Call:

"Submit totally to the Will of God...
and...
"Pray to be worthy to serve His Cause."

She rose unsteadily to her feet
shaking off an inexplicable dizziness.
Body and soul split apart
seemed to slowly re-unite
How much time had elapsed?
Was it seconds or hours
that she was catapulted to the shores of eternity?

The realization then slowly dawned
as she walked out in the strangest daze
that of His glory and might
she knew nothing yet,
or the essence of Faith itself.

Having felt less
than an atom of that all-swaying Spirit,
how could she ever
know fear?

Haifa, 2001

THE RESCUE

White, satin soft, glossy form
bedraggled and cold,
a slight shade of pink
in the harsh sunlight,
mottled and streaked
like some deadly disease.

Dark brown, sticky pods protrude
like the train of a bridal gown.
Powerful gliders that propel
to such dizzy heights,
carry it no further than a weak, lame duck.

It falls repeatedly on its stomach
as it struggles in pitiful flight,
there by the turning wheels
and narrow footpath.

One sharp swoop,
a forked hold,
an ignominious pose
and the trauma of liberation begins.

Its proud head twists from side to side.
Panic-filled, jet-black eyes
ringed by dark eyebrows
give a fierce, piratical look.

Hands, clumsy at first,
pluck and pull, fumble and tear,
probing for the tiny hooks
embedded deep in the winged carrier
that propagates through its movement
and even death,
the eternal cycle of rebirth.

It jabs at its liberators with dark yellow, curved beak
that can slice soft flesh with one sharp click.
The pressure behind the head is unrelenting.
The beak opens in silent terror
as the pods fall softly to the ground
in a tiny heap of fluff.
The skin of the underside is stretched and taut.
It twists anew, defiant to the last.
The more delicate snow white angels of paradise
do not survive this ordeal.

Twisted balls of feather, glued together by the pods,
evidence of its own desperate pecks
are left to the last.
Two hands are better than one
as we reach for the tiny hooks
and the path of least resistance.

The tense body trembles in agony
and the thin warm skin of the webbed feet
grow deathly cold to the touch.
Wings beat your arms relentlessly
 as feet jerk and kick in terror.

Eyelids flicker frantically as eyes close
in simulation of death.

And then you reach for the sky,
there by the shore
where the spray fills your nostrils.
You toss it high in the air
as the sun dips behind the horizon,
watch it fly out to sea;
far, far away from the treacherous shore.
Watch it disappear against the white canopy
of clouds,
heading straight for neighbouring Cousin,
from whence it came.

Perhaps it may visit our shores again this season.

2005

ALBERT AND MARJORIE

PART 1

Albert feeds on the overgrown lawn,
Marjorie, at the opposite end.
Albert crawls towards her–
all 287 kilos of manhood–
in a sudden burst of desire;
holds his scaly head so close to hers,
pretending yet to graze.
Loving yet quite discreet,
he circumambulates very slowly
to catch her undivided attention.
He fails!

He nudges her with his front leg,
his unique saddle shape touching hers,
badly scarred by an axe
during years of captivity on Praslin.
She grows very still, obviously unimpressed
by these intimate gestures.
Did she get the message or was she merely playing coy?
He stretches his neck as far as it can go.
Is it a cry of despair or a last appeal?

He continues his circular motion but heck!
A sapling has gotten in the way.
He can't edge her out of the way

For that would seem too pushy –
might put her off altogether.
He feeds instead close to her hind leg
in endearing slow motion.
She ignores him!

He pulls in his head as far as it can go.
Oh heck!
He can't believe his eyes!
She moves purposefully away
to feed on the opposite end of the lawn.
What a glutton!

He stares at her for a long moment.
Could she change her mind in the end?
No hope in hell!
How could she reject him so
when he followed all the rules?
Might as well continue to feed and hope for better days.

After all he has survived some 180 million years
and the mating season has only just begun.

PART 2

Later that day, Albert looks up in total disbelief.
Marjorie crawls right back.
She remains quite still, utterly submissive.
He tucks in his head.
Is he playing hard to get or merely digesting
this incredible stroke of luck.

He needs no further bidding as he mounts her sideways
trying to work his way around.
It takes quite a while to turn a full 45 degrees,
hind legs leaving a trail of crushed grass.
He grunts and snorts like a ship's horn
blasting its way to port.

He supplicates, his scaly head dangling over hers,
mouth wide open and dripping mucus.
He tries so hard to keep his grip,
clambering with flailing legs
as he keeps dropping heavily to the ground.
He is over three times Marjorie's 67 kilos.
Could that be the problem?
He tries over and over again, everything in readiness
but her back just won't rise or maybe it can't.

She grows weary of the unrelenting pressure
and tries to edge away but he hangs on desperately.
She succeeds to disengage herself at last
and moves quickly away.
Too tired to resist, Albert yawns and continues to feed.

Successful coition on Cousine is a mere 1%
but we have never felt such empathy
for a frustrated male in our entire life
and never more thankful
for humanity's shell-free moments of bliss.

2007

THE PAINTER

My father was a drunk, my mother always said,
till one fine day with some old mate,
he spurned the bridal bed,
and left us to our fate.

My mother she fell sick, my younger sisters moved
to a better home they said,
but we were left behind to prove
that I was ten, my brother twelve and household head.

We revelled in the freedom from dreary rules and chores,
playing games of wealth and fame,
till weeks turned into months and paint peeled off the doors,
yet no one ever came.

We tired of bread and coke and golf clubs up the hill
that earned us shiny coins for only one good aim—
to scrape a rare good meal,
still no one ever came.

My brother, he left school in search of some odd job
to see me through the years and success try to find,
but never once complained or heaved a sob
for what he left behind.

It was a rainy Monday, when I could plainly see
the guarded iron gates of sprawling NYS,

where I could be whatever I wanted to be,
and make some sense of this right old mess.

Some returned from home after week-ends out
with snacks to stack the shelves so bare
while I, not even toothpaste had to flout
or a single change of underwear.

So often I'd be scolded, punished and derided
for playing truant yet again,
that it was for the best, I then decided
to drop out altogether and live on like a man.

My brother joined the army, and I a great, big farm,
but then I turned to painting homes and office blocks,
till one day I intend, with sleeve rolled up my arm,
to open my own business, tending special crops.

After all I did endure,
I shall now become a dad,
but of one thing I am sure,
I'll give him all the love I never, ever had.

2006

BEHIND THE DESK

To speak or not to speak that is the question,
for to speak one's mind is mere foolish prattle,
but to dare make mention of some strange solution
is the threat of strong volition.

He treats every single thing
as strictly confidential
so when the phone rings,
he knows it's providential.

To do or not to do
that is also the question,
for even the little that he does
makes others oh, so glum!

To wait or not to wait
is a dilemma great
but he does not hesitate
or even vacillate.

Cherishing a secret hope
of a change at last,
with the present he copes
by repeating all that's past.

He never wears his patience thin
or gets to thinking for himself,

committing life's no greater sin than assuming
that creativity is performance's main ingredient.

To feel or not to feel
is the test of his manhood.
Emotion is his Achilles' heel–
hallmark of the female brood–

so if one jumps the tiresome queue,
with promises of such high return,
he does not stand up for the others few
that pass by empty palms upturned.

To plan how not to plan
is the new-found chaos theory
adopted by this humble servant,
growing oh so very weary!

But it suits him just as well,
to deal with case by case,
just watching for the sign
of the battle-weary line.

To be trained is to toss
in the seas of fantasy.
Re-engineering by the boss,
the cause of so much fuss!

Empowerment makes him queasy
for little do they know,
that seeds of doubt do sow,

of the relics of a distant past;

of the culture of patronage
and micro-island heritage,
such an age-old adage
adapted for the present age.

Many pressures he does bear,
fighting for the common share,
justifying every single means
by some noble ends unseen.

His re-organizations rare
are another let-down or a giant shake-down,
for some in need of a scare,
have gradually grown too big for their own.

Others need a size too small.
The seeds of discomfort yield rich harvests at fall
but the blind just can't see the significance of it all
for the common weal.

2000

GOING HOME

I lay on my back, gasping for air. They stood in a ring and looked down menacingly. There were six of them. I was vastly outnumbered as I lay there in the middle of the inner circle, partly hidden from view. I heard someone laugh viciously and braced myself for what was still to come. I tried desperately to shield my face from the full impact of a shiny, black, leather boot. My head suddenly whipped from side to side and the whole world was a giant carousel. The covered drain by the roadside lay only a few feet away. I had a sudden urge to crawl inside like the vermin that infested it. One of them gave a loud laugh and then they all disappeared as suddenly as they had appeared on that winter's day. The sound of mockery filled the air long after they had gone.

I raised my head slightly and through the pain I could see the stream of people passing me by, in the grey and black of winter. The great revolving doors kept turning incessantly in great semicircles beneath the gigantic letters that spanned the entire globe. Across the road, beautiful cashmere all the way from India lay on permanent display beside the open stalls that overflowed into the main street. I could almost touch the bright red pillar box that used to lie in the open pages on my mother's knees. I could feel at my back the rush of wind displaced by the towering red double-decker buses that carried the oppressed, trapped between the frills of conventionality and the open flood-gates of the electronic age.

I closed my eyes and woke up to the sound of a soft, gentle voice that was filled with concern.

"Are you badly hurt?"

"... Feel sore as hell," I mumbled.

"What's your name?" the voice persisted.

The letters rose from an ancient bark in a vision of utter darkness. The glorious promise ended in a desert of hopelessness until the children reaped of the seeds sowed by a wayward generation. I had longed for the city sidewalks and the taste of unfamiliar sights and sounds. I longed to float in a sea of strange faces, and listen to the grand orchestra of human emotion.

"Daniel," I whispered

"Where' you from?"

Oceans and continents ripped apart for a forgotten Eden. From the hidden depths, we lay uncharted in the blue silence across a zone of utter tranquillity. I am ultimately the fruit of the union of subjugation, that flowered before the cries of the wounded and crack of the whips faded beneath the last sunset. My roots are embedded in the soil of human indifference. Beneath the branches, the chorus ushers in the dawn.

"Seychelles," I answered.

"How lovely! Must be like living in paradise. Here's the stretcher. Hey, take it easy!"

Through the windows of the speeding ambulance, the large sidewalks appeared to narrow, chipped with age and broken in places. The growing corporations, with their French colonial roofs and plastered walls that kept peeling in the same places dwindled in size. The small range of commodities on the open shelves offered little choice and a far less complex buying process. The inquisitive faces hemmed you in from all sides, as you sauntered around the few buildings that made up the town centre. Sometimes they whispered to each other as you passed by.

Suddenly, the ambulance screeched to a halt and as I was carried out, I heard her speak again.

"You'll be taken in for observation, but not to worry–doesn't look like anything's broken."

I was discharged a few days later. Although badly bruised, I did not suffer from any broken bones. The doctor said that I was very fortunate indeed. I spent a few days with a friend and then returned to the London College to complete my studies. I graduated the following year and returned home in the autumn. I had the necessary qualifications to enter the corporate world as a promising young executive.

I searched for my friends in vain. My thoughts were too profound to share or maybe they were yet unformed. They say the light has gone out. It doesn't burn as brightly–perhaps. It does not flicker as much either. Sometimes I chase the fleeting shadows with what I can furtively muster from the dingy back streets of my old home town. I often walk alone in the sun and rain and catch a glimpse of the rainbow over the distant hills, or watch the ocean pour over the golden rim, beyond the new horizon.

BELVÉDÈRE

The first time he saw her, she was standing beside the tiny graves that lay some distance from the Frangipani tree that was in full bloom. The mounds of earth were still soft and moist. A single, white, ceramic tile lay in the centre, on which a small statue of the Madonna kept constant vigil. A birthday card was propped up against each small bouquet of wild flowers. The number of years on one of the cards had been carefully altered as the older boy would have turned four some months before. The card had been given to him on his third birthday.

Someone called out her name. She turned and saw him. He had phoned the day before and she was expecting him. She climbed the steep slope to meet him. He gazed curiously at the woman behind the headlines. She looked rather unkempt. She was tall, coffee-coloured and in her mid-thirties. Her hair was tied back in a thick plait. Her short, frilly dress swayed from side to side when she walked. She threw a frivolous comment over her shoulder as she passed by. Some staff from the Public Utilities Corporation, who were working nearby called her *'la folie'*–the madcap.

They walked past a magnificent view of the inner islands on that cloudless morning. A large cruise ship was anchored just outside Victoria harbour. Several yachts skimmed the blue surface as they captured for our peak season visitors the magic of paradise. Mount Copolia's sheer rock face towered to their left, dark, forbidding and forever in shadow. As they reached the little office above the cemetery, she went in to change from her working clothes. She reported there every day as part-time cemetery attendant on a special welfare scheme. Meanwhile, he paid a visit to the house just visible from the roadside.

It stood in a clearing, grim and strangely defiant. It had a well-demarcated boundary. He gazed in amazement at the number of houses hemming it in from all sides. He had somehow imagined a far more isolated spot. The house was tiny and built entirely of corrugated iron sheets–even the doors and windows. The windows were kept in place by some wooden bolts. He approached and tried to peep in through the gaps between the sheets. He detected the charred remnants of a chamber pot and a cooking pot. The burnt-out leg of a wooden cabinet that must have once been the centre of activity, stood against the wall. An iron bedpost lay in ruins at the far end. This must have been concealed behind a makeshift partition that afforded some vestige of privacy in that tiny shack.

The small yard outside was littered with natural debris that the heavy rains had deposited from the hillside. Houses continued to be built along the mountain slopes without adequate drainage facilities. Those living on lower ground had to face the constant invasion from above. One could well imagine the worms wriggling out of the rubbish and eating at the very fabric of that small community with its gossip and slander.

One of the children had been chronically sick. The doctor could not diagnose the cause of the mysterious ailment. He wanted to operate on his little heart. The mother had categorically refused. No one attributed it to the ill-kept secrets of a daily trauma.

There was no running water, bathroom or toilet facilities, as far as he could see. A few nailed sheets in the yard showed that work had started on one, but it remained unfinished. Water was obtained from a river, a tap by the roadside or a neighbour's house—whichever was the best option at the time. There was no electricity either. A neighbour had permitted her an electrical connection so that she could keep a refrigerator. This was illegal of course. It also posed a great danger to the inhabitants.

A single banana tree seemed to be the only living thing around. Its leaves were fresh and green. The surrounding earth had been recently weeded. A heavy bunch of bananas threatened to snap the tree trunk but someone had promptly supported it with a bamboo pole. It would be ripe for harvest in a week or so.

As he made his way back, the neighbours slowly emerged from their houses and stood near the path.

"Terrible thing to happen!" one of them muttered.

They were very anxious to explain how they had all tried to help in different ways.

"I liked the children," one young woman volunteered. "Often they would come home. They were always hungry. I'd offer them some food. Sometimes I'd look after them when she went out, but she was always out gallivanting. I couldn't do it all the time you see! I have children of my own, don't you see? I've got my own responsibilities. Some neighbours...relatives of hers, also took care of the children."

"We saw them alone at times, running on the road" added a middle-aged woman. "It wasn't safe."

"Did the authorities know about this?" he enquired.

"We notified the police and social agencies. After that, she would leave them locked up alone in that sweltering house. All the doors and windows were closed. It must have been like an oven in there. They would bang on the door for hours on end but we just couldn't do anything. She would get mad at us."

He had heard that she had as many as ten illegitimate children, but gave them all away. Two were at the St. Elizabeth orphanage. She denied this adamantly and only acknowledged the existence of the two at the orphanage but no-one believed her. The grandmother of the youngest child was very fond of him. She wanted to adopt him. The mother refused. He would have been alive if she had accepted the offer. Some people even said that she did it out of spite because the natural father had left her for another woman. No-one believed that either.

Another neighbour was less sympathetic.

"She didn't treat the kids well at all. She'd often beat them up when she came home. We would hear them crying. We were all fed up! We tried to counsel her to put some money aside or get some help from the district administration office and buy some building materials instead of squandering her money. She even bought a second hand television set that she couldn't even use! She had some strange priorities. Just before the fire, her long-outstanding application for government low-cost housing had come through. She was offered a much coveted, semi-detached, two bedroom house at the Roche Caiman housing estate. She never even went! She must be crazy!"

"Why didn't she go?"

"How would we know? All she had to do was to sign the loan agreement and fetch the keys. The kids would have been so much more comfortable there!"

She was not on speaking terms with almost everyone around the neighbourhood. Quarrels would often break out over some petty gossip, so they all left her to her own devices.

Pride, he gathered, was a luxury the poor could ill afford. When you had nothing left to give however, you could still give of your own flesh and blood. As the war of words escalated, the barricades went up.

He looked around that crowded neighbourhood. He felt suddenly cold at the thought of the tragedy that took place a few metres from where they were standing. The real horror suddenly struck him like a bolt of lightning.

"Surely", he asked, "some of you must have noticed something that day!"

An old lady standing a few feet away startled us all.

"I was there when it happened."

She pointed to a banana tree that stood just inside the boundary.

"I spoke to the children locked up in the house. There was some commotion. The older boy was blaming his brother for something that had happened. He kept repeating, *'Ou sa, ou sa!'* (It's you, it's you!) Then I heard screams. I asked them what they were up to. They didn't reply. I don't know if they heard me."

"But surely the screams of those kids must have been ghastly!" he persisted. "It must have truly alarmed you at some point."

He had heard from some neighbours further uphill that the children had screamed and screamed and people working as far away as the cemetery and right up the hill could hear them. A loud explosion was also heard. Some thought it could have been a petrol stove bursting–or the children's' heads.

"I did hear a terrible scream at one point," the old lady admitted sheepishly, "but then there was complete silence."

"Didn't any of you see any smoke that could have alerted

you as to the gravity of the situation?"

Apparently, none of them saw any smoke from where they were standing. The relatives, who lived at the back however, were the first to detect the smoke emerging from the roof. They alerted the fire brigade. It was mid-morning by the time they arrived. The fire must have started at around nine o'clock and not long after Jeanne had left the house.

"Have you any idea what caused the fire? he inquired.

"Can't say for sure," the younger woman said. "She could have left something on the fire. She did that sometimes. Some people even say that she started the fire herself because she wanted to be rid of them. I don't believe that though."

He thanked them for all their help and slowly made his way back to the car. Jeanne was ready and waiting beside the vehicle.

"You've seen how I live now," she snapped. "I have been asking the government for decent housing for thirteen years. People better off than me have received housing assistance before me. I tried to obtain some bricks and cement from the district office. When I finally received them, my damn relatives wouldn't allow me to construct a bathroom and toilet behind my house. They said that I was intruding on their property."

It seemed that the relatives who lived in their solid, brick houses fought bitterly over a few feet of family backyard. This came as no surprise. Cases relating to boundaries or *balizaz,* as they are commonly known, have pre-occupied the civil courts for almost a century and probably created more problems in the land than the two world wars put together. Those who accused her of negligence or promiscuity had never experienced the pangs of abandonment for lack of a toilet bowl or running water. The way she spent her welfare cheque also displeased those who earned in one month the sum total of all her earthly possessions. These were valued at sixteen thousand Rupees–lock, stock and barrel. As they drove away, he asked her about the housing offer that she had not taken up.

"How could I?" she retorted. "It's a very expensive house for someone of my means. Do you know how much the loan repayment is per month? They are moreover insisting that people pay the full amount and don't default. I had urged them on several occasions to give me cheaper lodgings at Les Mammelles. I had even identified a vacant apartment and seen the Member of Parliament in my district. She was very unhelpful and rude. That infuriated me and I lashed out at her."

They reached their destination. As they walked down the corridor, some of the office staff who were around stared in surprise. She held her head up high.

As they settled in, she continued, "I earn only eight hundred Rupees per month. The father of the kids contributes three hundred and fifty for the children. It isn't much. I can't even afford day care. I can't ask him for more because I know he doesn't earn very much himself. I tried to supplement my income by taking on another part-time job taking care of an old woman who lived close by. She gave me six hundred per month for a couple of hours work in the morning. I would reach there at six, before the children woke up and return by eight in the morning. I used to leave a bottle of milk for my kid before going to the cemetery. I'd return at break-time with some buns for tea. My children were well fed. They even had a choice of dishes. Macaroni was their favourite."

Her body stiffened in agony at the thought and then she broke down at the memory of the trivial detail. Her eyes quickly filled with tears and she trembled, toying agitatedly with the little wooden cross around her neck as she leaned forward on the upholstered sofa.

"It was terrible! I suffered dreadfully you know."

"Of course," he said, "but you can't bring them back now. The least you can do is to make something better of your life.

"They did not want me to see the corpses," she continued, as if he had not spoken. "I forced them to uncover the little bodies. Their teeth were tightly clenched. I was hysterical, and had to be hospitalized for several months. I still see him every night–my older son. I haven't had a decent night's sleep since it happened. I always have the same dream. He appears suddenly and beckons me to follow him deep into the woods. When I start to dig in the very spot that he points to, he disappears in a thick smokescreen. Michel, my elder son, used to tell me not to leave him alone with his younger brother. I never paid attention. Perhaps he had been warning me about something. Maybe he still is!"

She sank back into the sofa as she re-lived her torment. He remembered reading how devastating the fire was. All that was left of them were some charred remains that had to be carried out in a shovel. So tender were their years that they had burrowed for freedom in the very heart of the inferno. They were found crouching under an old wooden cabinet, cowering under a prized school bag. Afterwards, all that could identify them was their teeth, tightly clenched in their last moments of writhing agony.

As he poured coffee, her profound sadness gave way to a deep bitterness that welled up from deep within.

"The children got on well together. I couldn't separate them by giving one away. Wouldn't you have done the same?"

As this was more of a rhetorical question, she did not wait for an answer, nor did he venture one.

"Their quarrel was with me–not the innocent children. They say that I burned them alive. They are a malicious lot! There was nothing on the fire when I left for work that day. The matches were high up on a cabinet, well out of reach of the kids. I just can't understand it."

"Perhaps you forgot to put them away that day. You were in a hurry to go for a job interview at the duty free shop. There were some papers that you had to bring with you."

"They wouldn't have dared do anything naughty in my absence because they were afraid of the consequences. I had no choice but to frighten them by caning them. That kept them out of trouble. I thought they were safer in the house than outside. No one was prepared to look after them when I was away. They were once seen running across the road while they were in someone *else's* care. Anyway, I hear that there were some children playing around the house that day. Anyone could have lit a piece of paper and pushed it under the door."

The expression on his face must have told her that he thought this a rather far-fetched supposition.

"Isn't that highly unlikely?" he asked.

"If this was no malicious deed, then how come no one came to the rescue except the fire brigade?" she continued defiantly. "By then of course, it was too late. The door was locked but they could have easily broken it down. The neighbours were home and within a few feet of the scene. They did absolutely nothing. The blood of my children is on their hands. I will never forgive them."

"Did the police or authorities talk to you at all?" he asked curiously.

"Oh yes! They came once and asked me a lot of questions. I didn't see them again."

He knew then that he would never know the truth. The cause of the fire would be a secret that she would take with her to the grave. Maybe it was a mystery to her as well.

The room was suddenly grew terribly cold despite the sizzling temperature outside. They could not speak for a while. Then they talked for a little while longer. He hoped that the sacrifice of these babies would not be in vain. She could start to look for a steady job. After all, she had completed one year at the Polytechnic hotel school. She could even contemplate fetching her two sons from the orphanage to live with her. She immediately said that she didn't feel up to it yet and he did not press her.

They met twice after that. She needed some advice and help on each occasion. At one time, she was very upset about the possibility of losing the Roche Caiman house. The authorities considered it rather too big for a single person. He appealed to them and they allowed her to remain on humanitarian grounds.

He met her on the road once. She was well groomed. The clothes she wore were all donations she had received. She was completely lost in thought as she made her way to Anse Royale. She was apparently visiting a nun who was seeing her through those difficult times. She showed him some pictures of the new home that she had been furnishing. It looked so bright and warm. The children would have loved it! She was very proud of it too. She hadn't found a full time job yet. He didn't ask if she had been trying. She was still on welfare.

Months later, his secretary spotted her at a bus stop. She had a new-born baby in her arms. He couldn't believe his ears!

Apparently, her new neighbours had lodged complaints about her to the authorities. The exact nature of the problem was unclear. A social worker later told him that the baby had bruises on his body. It had occurred during the mother's absence. Some said that her new boyfriend was baby-sitting at the time. She had also tried to take her sons from the orphanage but the sisters of the Convent had refused. They were about to be adopted by a cousin of hers.

He has not seen her since that day. Once however, he was shown a newspaper article about an incident that had occurred at the graveside of the children. Two older children from a former relationship had appeared to put some flowers on the grave of the half-brothers whom they had never known. A bitter row broke out. The children simply wanted her to acknowledge their existence. She refused and denies all knowledge of them to this day. Heart-broken but determined, they refuse to give up.

After a while, life went on as usual. The incident became, like so many others, just a distant memory. Visits to the two tiny graves became more and more infrequent. He still hears those terrible screams that went unheard. He sees two tiny bodies burrowing inside a wooden cabinet and cowering under a precious school bag in a last desperate attempt to escape. The flames and smoke engulf the cluttered hut but there is no exit. The world outside is completely shut out. The silence that follows seems to go on... and on... and on... He believes that there is a special place under the shadow of the wings of God for all those little ones. There was never any trial. There was no court of law; no defendant, prosecutor or jury. The burden of truth may lay many feet underground, beside a small hill slope covered with white and yellow blossoms. It may be buried deep in every human heart, where innocence and guilt have made strange bedfellows, ever since Eve's taste for knowledge surpassed the bounds of human possibility.

SOUTHERN SEAS

The smell of cinnamon fills the air. A few tree stumps lie by the footpath. They are a constant reminder of a thriving industry in an unsophisticated land. The slim branches of the tall Trumpet Trees weave a thick green mesh that keeps away the scorching heat and awakens you to the dusky sights of a perennial autumn below. A rare grass snake slithers from the path and burrows through a heap of mouldering leaves. The Banyan Tree wraps the giant boulder in a life-giving embrace, as her roots twine down in search of scarce nutrients from the soil beneath. The termites nest in full view as they parasitically live off the helpless trunk of a maturing tree. The familiar sound of the forest stream cannot be heard. The parched soil has sucked her up, drop by drop, in the gathering heat. Beside the path, the yellow, translucent tips of several stakes are driven firmly into the ground at regular intervals. They pave the way for things to come. The tall casuarinas shed their silken brown hair where the dark green mountain forests joins the undulating, lime green slopes of Beach Morning Glory that grip the sand in a desperate effort to withstand the fierce seasonal onslaught.

The sea spray suddenly fills our nostrils as we approach an unbroken stretch of beach, occasionally disturbed by turtles that drag themselves up the beach to lay their eggs, oblivious of the marauders that lurk in the shadows. At the near end, the beach meets the dried up river mouth in a towering cliff of sand that makes a delightful ski-run, as we tumble headlong in complete abandon. Some weathered fragments of turtle shell are half-buried in the sand–the remnants of the rapacious exploits of the poachers of *Petit Boileau.*

The dark grey cluster of rocks far out to sea will face the onrushing waves for countless centuries before they also lie on the coral bed, to be washed up in denuded fragments and exposed one day on the far side of the beach when the south-east monsoon carries the surface sand across the headland to the adjacent bay.

As the sun starts to set, the mountain sways in shades of green and gold as the first bats hover close to their craggy homes and we make our way across the beach to the other hillside. The path is flanked by myriads of small coconut palms and strewn with scorched palm leaves and germinating fruit. Here we savoured of the tasty *koko zerm* and quenched our thirst while the children spilled most of it down their shirts. We never climbed very far. The stories of strange happenings were still fresh in our minds.

At the rocky pools, the multitude of tiny coloured fishes dart in and out of rocks, studded with rock crabs and laden with limpets. The children spend hours feeding the fishes as they shelter from the thunderous fountains of sea spray rising from the huge breakers that crash just a few metres away. Tucked away between the rocks, an experienced eye can detect the outer shell of a mother-of-pearl. The dark grey head of a young eel pops in and out of the safety of its dark crevasse but never ventures very far from home.

The upper part of the beach is covered with Beach Morning Glory. A few bits of timber are all that's left of the old hut in which Dan and Zakari spent many years. They were accompanied by an old cow tethered to a coconut tree and covered in sea spray and flies. The ruins of the outer stonewalls of an old coconut dryer are just visible from the shore. In former days, the kiln was used to make copra for export. It was built of granite rock, red earth and coral, some forty years ago. There were four holes that acted as air vents. The coconut would be spread on top of the flat roof and dried by the heat generated inside the dryer. The roof had disappeared but it was a mobile one. It had rails so that when it rained the coconuts would be covered. When the sun shone, the roof would slide back. This would eventually be the site of the new restaurant, serving the clients in the chalets along the hillside and the large villa at the top. Just below the dryer was a heap of rocks–the remnants of a fireplace in the old house that was built in the forties to accommodate the workers. It had a thatched roof and walls. The inhabitants lived on fish, breadfruit and rice. The administrator, Charlemagne Hoareau, also lived there for a while, followed by Expedi Mondon's father.

"I lived here for seven years," Expedi explained. "Every day I walked all the way to Takamaka School and back. It was a hell of a trek! I had to wake up at five in the morning. Do you know why? Rats! Yeah, rats! I had to catch them in my rat trap before going to school. Have you seen what one looked like? Here, Xavier will show you."

The trap was made of bamboo with a lasso inside. The rat would trigger the noose upon entrance and hang itself.

"We worked terribly hard. Work was assigned or measured by bamboo lengths. You had so many bamboo lengths to clear, weed or plant in a day. We produced vanilla, cinnamon and coconut. Cinnamon was distilled in our three distilleries here but we sent the vanilla to Anse Royale and the copra to Adam Moosa for export. We produced 50,000 nuts per month!"

In 1955, Expedi's father transferred to *Petite Anse* where he lived for eleven years. Following in the footsteps of his father, Expedi returned to *Petit Boileau* and worked as administrator.

We were inevitably joined by Francois and his mistress, her grandchild and their brown dog. He must have spotted the car parked at the top.

"Marie will make you a lovely curry of *bernik*. She is a very good cook."

"That's great. It's been a long time since I've eaten any. It mustn't be too spicy though."

"Sure!" he answered, looking longingly out to sea. "We can't fish at all these days, even from the rocks. It's too dangerous.

"What do you catch around here?"

"Oh, all sorts–*bourgeois, vieille...*"

"Any sharks? I asked in trepidation, thinking of our bathing sprees during the north-east and the absence of any protective ring of reefs.

"Oh no, never, never any sharks!" he assured us.

François was a coxswain who had settled down with a woman much older than him and who was already a grandmother. The beautiful little grand-daughter had been virtually adopted by her when she found that her daughter had been neglecting the child.

As we left the beach, Marie confided in me. "It's very difficult for us without a telephone and transport. What would happen in the case of an emergency? My little girl has to walk one mile to the bus stop every day in order to get to school. Sometimes she gets a lift from the boss on his way from work. That's a big help."

"All this will change when the tourism development project gets under way," I tried to re-assure her.

I later found out that François had been employed as a single guy. In due course however, the members of two generations accompanied him. With the usual flexibility associated with a certain degree of island compassion and humanitarianism, the employers had turned a blind eye and allowed the family to live off the land. Francois was paid a small basic salary as watchman.

The next time we visited, the winds were blowing from the north-west and south-west. Francois had been dismissed. William and old Melo were on the hill-top tending the garden. Melo was sixty-six years old but he would be up on the dance floor with his young wife before anyone else. They were both children of the soil and knew every inch of the place. William's father and grandfather had been administrators and managers of the property. In those days they were called *komander*. Old Melo's earliest memories of the owners dated back to the time of Felix Dingwall, alias Féfé.

"When he died, the property was owned by two sisters," he explained. "One of them was looked after by Mr Mondon. She bequeathed everything to him before her death. She had outlived her sister. I used to live here with my mother but I collected coconuts over the other side, at *Grand Police*."

"What did your mother do?"

"Many things," he answered proudly. "She removed cinnamon bark and also made flour from tapioca. She would crush it manually in the big wooden grinder. The school children loved it. Did you know," he added, "that I was one of the first to work on the Melitoma project? Do you know how many trees we planted? Two thousand, two hundred and forty eight!"

His memory for figures was quite astounding. It must have been imprinted in his mind for several decades! It was little wonder that the whole area was densely covered with coconut palms. I had thought that they were part of the original landscape. The disease must have ravaged the coconut plantation and threatened copra production in a significant way.

Old Melo finally got down to preparing a meal for the dogs on an open fire. William meanwhile showed us the alternative way to the beach. They had just cleared it. It was still very steep but much wider in most places. It ended right behind the site of the future restaurant and chalets. This meant that a large part of the foreshore to the right could remain virtually undisturbed. It was a delightful thought!

I discovered the main river that gushed down the mountain and the little rock pool beneath the large Dragon's Blood tree, better known as *Sandragon* and the *Vouloutier* or Half Flower, their leaves all withered up by the sea spray. We bent low to drink the crystal cool, unchlorinated water and could see the dark grey rocks lurking beneath.

At the beach, we found that the wind and currents had eroded it at one end and deposited the load at the opposite end. A deep valley was formed and a cliff of sand imprinted with patterns that resembled those of the Grand Canyon, towered above us. The familiar marsh had disappeared as the river flowed unhindered through the valley and into the sea. It was astonishing to see the sea looking so tame. The reflection of the mid-day sun on the glittering sands forced you to turn towards the more soothing green landscape. It was then that we noticed the trail of footprints that disappeared behind the rocks. The second set of tracks was no human footprints but those of a well-protected species of reptile–the hawksbill turtle. Its flippers had left two distinct sets of tracks; one marking its laborious ascent and the other its descent. One could tell the difference by the angle of the tracks. We followed them to the top of the beach. The sand had been recently dug up in several places. We dug excitedly where the sand appeared to be softest. We were very careful not to harm any of the eggs that could be hidden away. All we knocked against however, were the roots of the plants that had gradually crept down the beach. The mother must have made several unsuccessful attempts to lay her burden down and finally lumbered off to some other shore. It couldn't have been the roots that posed an obstacle because her flippers were so powerful that they could tear them apart with one deft movement. Perhaps the sand was too soft and the walls had collapsed repeatedly.

We clambered up faster than we had ever done before in order to keep up with our guide who sauntered up effortlessly. I couldn't control my heavy breathing, which I was sure could be heard by all. When we reached the top, I felt quite faint and even had to bend my head quite low to steady myself. The old man was still around and this time he pointed to the mountain side that had hitherto remained unexplored. We heard some amazing stories that sent shivers down our spine.

"The young boy who was employed last year stayed only three days. He was clearing the vegetation up there when he heard a sharp whistle. He felt himself lifted up into the air by an invisible force and then thrown down forcibly. I myself was sitting right here in the clearing with William and Expedi when we heard some voices. They were those of a mother and her children. They seemed to be coming from below. We all went to investigate. We looked everywhere but couldn't find anyone. It was most uncanny!"

"Sounds can be very deceptive, you know," my very scientific husband quickly explained, "especially near the sea. The wind can magnify voices that in actual fact come from a great distance. It depends on the direction in which the wind is blowing."

They both looked totally unconvinced. William had his own tales of the supernatural.

"I was walking over there alone. There was no one around. Suddenly I felt hot ash on my back as though someone had thrown it with great anger–man–was it scary! I remember a guy who was helping us cut and dry the leaves of the Thief Palms. He took the path by the beach to reach *Grand Police* bay when he felt his bundle grow lighter and lighter until it seemed that he was carrying nothing. He was so scared that he disappeared and never came back–not even to get his money. Xavier had made himself a cup of tea by the clearing near the beach. He was alone. He returned after a minute and saw a huge pebble in his cup. Brandishing his long knife, he challenged the intruder in the dark. I tell you - no one was there!"

I did not want to say that these may all have been pranks played by someone who wanted them out of the way. He looked so mysterious as though he was holding something back and words could never fully convey the sense of fear and excitement. Most of this happened when the road was being constructed in 1994.

"The old watchman, who lived by the beach, heard Zachari call out to him from under the rocks in the middle of the night."

"Who on earth was Zachari? I asked. The name evoked images of inhabitants from another age.

"He was the old watchman who lived most of his life on the property. He is dead now but his spirit haunts the place."

"I have been here many times," I said, "but I have never experienced any of these bizarre encounters. The only thing we heard once was a sharp whistle. We attributed that to some kind of bird."

They looked at me strangely as though they shared something that could never be divulged. Anyway, I didn't want to argue too much. It certainly shrouded the place in an aura of mystery. The sudden silence was broken.

"Can Xavier take us to the *basen diri*?" I asked, bringing them abruptly back to earth.

"Of course, but you'd better set off now as it may take over an hour to get there and back."

We climbed the hill beside the water wells and soon reached a small house in the clearing. It was surrounded by breadfruit and banana trees and a small stream trickled down the mountain side. The water looked clean enough to drink as there was no habitation beyond. The place was rebuilt of plywood and corrugated iron in 1997. The steep roof was covered with coconut leaves. The only original thing left was the nine pillars made of heaped rocks. The old house once had a roof of palm leaves and walls. It had a small living room and two tiny bedrooms. Up to six people or a whole family used to live there.

The woods leading to the rice basin were thick with palms and vanilla trees. Very little sunlight could penetrate. Palm leaves still lay on the ground to dry. Some had recently been sold to an architect.

"Look," shouted Xavier. "They are already sprouting new leaves. It's pretty fast as it has not even been a year. Perhaps where more sunlight gets through, growth is faster–who knows?"

Everywhere, we could see little saplings growing where the ripe pods had cast their seeds. Wild vanilla, like dark green serpents wound their way round tree trunks, held to the ground by a couple of very thin roots. Suddenly we were in the wide open space, the sunlight dazzling our droopy eyes. A huge overhanging, granite plateau stretched out before us, sloping down to the mountain edge and offering a spectacular view of *Grand Police* and the old prison. The rain at sea looked like a motionless spout or a mist from heaven. And then we finally saw what we had come for. Its name was scrawled in white paint on the rocks. Hardly more than one and a half metres in diameter and nestling at the lower end of the granite outcrop was a small oval basin containing some rich, dark moist earth and only three dozen rice plants. This was what all the fuss was about! Theories were rife as to how they got there. Selwyn clung tenaciously to his bird theory.

"Rice was planted in the Seychelles a long time ago in marshy areas. A bird could have dropped a grain in this particular spot."

I had the human hand theory.

"On the other hand, someone sitting in this very same spot could have experimented by throwing some grains of rice in this moist earth to see if it could grow."

Xavier had absolutely no theory.

"I just don't know," he repeated time and time again. He sat there looking down and reminiscing.

"Do you see that little beach partly hidden by the casuarinas trees? We call it *P'ti Polis*. From here, I have seen turtles come up at 10 am. to lay their eggs."

"How bad was the *Tsunami* here?"

"Gosh, was I scared that day! We were having a sort of picnic over there at *P'ti Polis*. It was around 12 pm. when I noticed a high tide. Hey, I thought, this was not normal. High tide was supposed to be at 5 am. Then suddenly, the sea seemed to run dry. I just couldn't believe what I saw. It was dry land up to almost thirty metres of water. Do you see that headland? We could see the rocks at the bottom of the sea there. They were huge. We stopped the music to listen to the radio. It was then that we heard of the Tsunami. I looked up and there was a helicopter and some army chaps were shouting at us to leave the beach. I was fishing by the rocks. I ran up in the nick of time, as seconds later I would have been swept out to sea. It was very weird. It did not come up like a wave. The sea seems to suddenly swell up and rise, sweeping everything in its path. All our picnic tables and chairs vanished in the twinkling of an eye."

As it was getting late, we made our way back to where the car was parked. My husband wanted some help with the nuts he had collected under the tree. I foraged for a bag in which to cart away the heap of *cajou*. They were dark brown and looked like giant kidney beans. Those on the tree were still suspended from their bright orange pods. The children had never seen them in their natural state. They were surprised that the actual nut was only a very small part of the fruit.

"You have to leave them out in the sun for a while to dry," old Melo explained. "Then you can roast them."

We finally bade everyone good-bye and drove off. The

memory of crackling leaves as we slithered down the mountain side was still vivid in my mind. I knew then, that the day was fast approaching when we would never be able to retrace our steps. When the road was built, we could never again capture the same magic of the wilderness.

FATSO AND POOT

They rushed excitedly into her bedroom that Sunday afternoon. They had just returned from a 'Bring and Buy' sale with their dad. They tugged at her arm.

"Close your eyes *manman*," cried Rieul, pulling her out of the chair. "Don't open them until you reach the garage!"

They succeeded in distracting her from the heaps of files and letters in front of her. Then she was suddenly overwhelmed by a familiar sinking feeling in the pit of her stomach. This was serious. She didn't like surprises. Her anxiety grew. She couldn't bear the suspense. She had to know!

"What is it?" she asked in trepidation. "Don't tell me it's another dog?"

She thought in dismay of the litter of corpses that were the hallmark of Bimbo's daily existence as he sought to satisfy his Rottweiler instinct by hunting in chicken coops, marshes, cages and footpaths all around the neighbourhood.

"No," they chorused in reply.

"Is it a tortoise?" she persisted.

"No."

It had to be something much worse. Mercifully the agonizing suspense was almost over.

"You can open your eyes now," they shouted in unison.

She stumbled to a halt at the end of the garage, opened her eyes and gazed in well concealed horror at the sight that confronted her. On top of the storage cabinets stood a neat little cage of wire mesh nailed to a wooden frame. It had a square door with a wooden knob. In it were two guinea pigs. They were white with black and brown patches and pink ears. On the floor were two tiny plastic bowls, one blue and one yellow. One was filled with water. In the other was a freshly peeled banana. The floor was strewn with fresh Guinea Grass, their favourite food.

"We've already given them names. This is Fatso," explained Rieul proudly pointing at the plump female sitting on its hind legs, nibbling hungrily at the banana. "The other is Poot."

Poot lay quietly at the back of the cage. She could swear that it gave her a positively mournful look. She ran her fingers gently down the side of the cage to show him that she understood.

"Aren't you surprised *manman*?" Tyrian cried, amazed at the long silence. For once she was speechless. She couldn't hurt their feelings but she wasn't all that good at faking either. Her voice came out flat and matter of fact.

"Who, may I ask, is going to look after them?"

"We are of course," they chimed.

Recollections of Bimbo's first year with them came flooding back. They bathed him every week and then every month. After that she had to remind them each time. Finally she forgot herself and poor Bimbo had to jump into the marsh sometimes to bathe himself, consoled only by the joy of hunting down some hapless tilapia. His wet, bedraggled figure would leave big puddles all over the veranda, attracting the few flies of the neighbourhood.

The most important question was left for last.

"Who on earth is going to clean their droppings?"

She had noticed how it would plop through the wire mesh

and plaster the concrete shelf beneath.

"We are of course."

At that point she directed an enquiring look at their dad who hovered on the sidelines, shuffling to and fro in ill-concealed apprehension. He attempted to pacify her and extricate himself from this predicament.

"They both wanted them so much! They made their own bids at the auction. In fact Rieul was so keen that he bid against himself several times."

"We paid three hundred Rupees for them," Tyrian added proudly, obviously still impressed by the enormity of the sum.

There was very little left to say. She entered the living room, and sank resignedly into the sofa.

It happened an hour later. The children were watching 'Hocus Pocus' on television. The parents were in the middle of a scrabble game–a Sunday afternoon ritual that lasted a few months and which always turned into a major competition. They armed ourselves with all the ammunition they could muster. They spent hours delving into the new English Oxford Reference and the Chambers Official Scrabble Lists to devise triple word scores. They were completely engrossed when Tyrian rushed in from the veranda, sobbing his little heart out–mind you–it wasn't always a cause for alarm. Most of the time it could be over something quite trivial. This time however his face had gone quite pale and his lips were turning blue.

"What's the matter?" they cried, rising to their feet, all dreams of triple word scores vanishing.

He could hardly get the words out but his eyes spoke of the horror that he had just witnessed. "Bimbo...he...he...he... killed ...them," he sobbed.

She froze. "Oh no!" they exclaimed in unison. She felt

completely helpless in the face of such a catastrophe. Nothing in the world, we knew, could console him at that moment.

Danger signals then flashed in her brain. 'Crisis!' she thought, 'Quite definitely a crisis–calls for great psychological sensitivity.' She remembered another incident in the family. Their cousins had recently lost their dogs. They had apparently been poisoned. I couldn't remember how they coped with that. All she knew was that the children cried their eyes out initially. That wasn't much help to her at that moment!

As they stepped onto the veranda, she caught a glimpse of Bimbo in the distance. "That monster!" she exclaimed vociferously, needing desperately to find a victim on which she could vent her annoyance, in the vague hope that anger might somehow dissipate sorrow.

They reached the end of the veranda and caught a glimpse of the tiny bundles that lay sprawled beside the local apple tree some distance from each other. She winced. She could not even bring herself to approach the scene of the crime. The children were already circling the area while their dad went about inspecting the cage which was concealed behind the car in the garage where it had fallen. Bimbo had obviously reached up on his hind legs and clawed it down from its heights. Rieul cried silently, his face all contorted in pain as he bent over each in turn caressing and fanning their little bodies with a large Takamaka leaf as if willing them back to life, or perhaps saying good-bye.

"How come we didn't hear any noise whatsoever?" she asked. "Sometimes I wish we wouldn't put the T.V. on so loud!"

This indirect accusation caused them to contemplate for a grave moment our own role in this hideous incident. Having done so they then started to sob even louder at the thought of how oblivious they had been of the suffering and pain of their little pets just a few moments before. Talk of making matters worse!

Then they caught a glimpse of a black and white dog disappearing behind my mum's house. Bimbo must have had an accomplice, a stranger! That was unbearable! She urged the kids to chase the dog away immediately. Then it suddenly dawned upon her that it probably wasn't such a good thing for the children to see their pets in that state but by then it was too late! Fatso was on its side, one eye open, and its little legs in mid air while Poot lay on its stomach. The fur around their necks was stained red where the canine teeth had sunk into the soft flesh. Tyrian had in fact earlier seen Bimbo with one of them in his mouth. They had already stomached every single detail and nothing could pull them away from the scene. On second thoughts, perhaps it was good to cry after all–a sort of cathartic experience. She finally made a thoroughly futile attempt to comfort them.

"They didn't suffer at all you know. Animals are not like humans. They have very small brains so they do not feel pain like we do. Before they were aware of anything it must have been all over for them."

Tyrian was totally unconvinced and gazed at her incredulously. "How silly can you be? They must have been terrified seeing this huge monster clawing at their cage and banging it about." The reminder that they were mere animals brought on a fresh outburst.

"They do not even go to heaven," Tyrian sobbed, remembering the conversation we had a few days earlier on the differences between man and beast. "They are completely finished!"

Then another more ghastly thought struck him. "We spent all our money for nothing!"

That was an easy one. She had a ready answer. "The money is not important. It was a contribution for a good cause. It goes into God's fund. Anyway we can get you other guinea pigs. There are loads in the country. You can even have rabbits if you prefer."

She rather liked the idea of rabbits. They seemed altogether more wholesome.

They were rather dubious. "We haven't seen any around. Anyway, I am sure they will never be as sweet as Fatso and Poot", Rieul added.

"Oh, rubbish! she exclaimed vigorously. "They could be much, much sweeter!"

They turned to their dad for immediate verification of facts, which he did with an almost imperceptible nod of his head.

She decided to distract then by engaging their energies in some creative activity.

"I suggest you bury them and give them some sort of funeral. Find something to demarcate their burial ground and print a few words or poem to place on the grave. Try to write a lovely poem, one straight from the heart."

This met with their instant approval. They rushed around with their dad, looking for the hoe and debating about a suitable spot for their resting place. Then they sat at their computer designing a colourful epitaph. The crisis was finally over.

"Come and see *manman*," they called from behind the house.

She stepped outside and discovered that they had buried them under the orange tree that had just begun to bloom but had never ever borne fruit. In the twilight, she could discern an old brick that marked the tragic spot. Stuck to it was an A-4 sheet bearing the fruits of their creativity. She rushed to the burial ground. She expected the epitaph to be quite astounding. It was indeed, but in a different sort of way.

HERE LIES
Fatso and Poot
our
beloved
guinea pigs

Sorry Fatso and Poot our 2 most beloved guinea pigs,
when I saw you, you meant to me a lot,

now I will get another pair of guinea pigs,
who don't drink from my pot
you know Fatso and Poot,
killing you I would not dare.
You know you have lots of fur,
but I call it hair.
Well I'm sorry you died,
you died in your cage.
But I know something about you,
you died in young age.
And Fatso and Poot,
I made a gravestone for you.
There's something I did not mind you did,
it was pooh.

Well this is what happened
it was night
something happened
when there was not a creak of light
a brave dog called Bimbo
stood up like a knight.
And something else
Bimbo was not in sight
that was when it happened
you died...
then what we did
was cry!

Fatso and Poot,
you were the cutest guinea pigs that I ever saw.
We love you very much.

The words were framed by myriad stars, hearts and suns in red, yellow and green. Rieul grew philosophical as he stared at this piece of art.

"Perhaps its better they died sooner rather than later. If we became so attached to them after a few hours–just imagine what it would have been like if we had lost them after some days!"

They couldn't have agreed more. "Moreover they can now be useful. They can enrich the soil and the orange tree may actually bear fruit." That didn't seem to whet their appetite for oranges!

A few minutes later, calm restored, the family was in the sitting room when their dad came in with some additional information about the incident.

"Bimbo is terrible! Do you know what he did? He tore a hole in the wire mesh and then went over to the other side of the fence to force them out so that he could enjoy chasing them before the kill."

"Please, that's enough!" she cried, dreading the outcome of this dreadful revelation. Sure enough Tyrian's face crumpled again. She dashed to the rescue, well prepared this time.

"Don't worry. They may have thought it was a game. They are not as intelligent as you or Bimbo."

"Of course not," Tyrian retorted disbelievingly. "They squeaked. They must have squeaked! They were scared." The memory of this last squeak seemed to rip his little heart out. It was a desperate cry for help that had gone unheard by their protectors and new masters.

After a few minutes however, he settled down again. She only hoped that they would forget their intentions of acquiring more guinea pigs as long as Bimbo was around. She was sadly mistaken!

One Sunday afternoon when the children had gone out to sea with their dad in a pedal boat and she was keeping her mum company on the beach close to the Reef hotel, Daniel, a friend, came quietly up.

"Where are the children? I have the guinea pigs they were interested in. Rama got in touch with a woman living up the mountain who has a whole breed of them. She has so many she doesn't know what to do with them."

She had no choice but to thank him for this very prompt and unexpected response to a crisis and followed him in complete resignation to the car. In the boot was a small carton box. He opened the top and she held my breath as she beheld Fatso and Poot scurrying about without a care in the world.

This time, they were much, much wiser. The cage was suspended high up on the metal rails of the water tank, well out of reach of Bimbo. The children went out every morning–or evening to scout for their favourite food around the yard. Very soon these were exhausted. They then had to go much further afield, beyond the big green gates and they had to scour the neighbourhood. Before long, they had an unexpected surprise!

One evening, they emerged sleepily from their rooms to find a litter of tiny bodies huddled against Poot and feeding voraciously. Danger loomed or so they were advised. Quickly, a partition went up between Fatso and Poot before the jealous male could crush and kill whatever stood in the way of his pleasure.

One month went by. The effort proved too much for the boys, despite all their good intentions. So one Sunday morning, down came the cage when Bimbo was well out of the way and off they all drove to Port-Glaud farm. Pat welcomed them and made no comment when he was offered Fatso and Poot back and a whole lot more, without any charge whatsoever. It was almost as though this was not an uncommon occurrence. Heaving a big sigh of relief, the boys made their way up the slope and then gasped as they beheld scores and scores of guinea pigs scurrying about in a giant pen. Their secret admiration for Pat knew no bounds. Now his animal farm would be complete and they could go back to the life they knew!

MONA

I remember my mother bringing me beautiful dresses. Her name was Sultana Shirazi. Her grandfather, Mihdi, was born in 1844 in the city of Shiraz. He was of holy lineage, a descendant of the Prophets. He was one of the early disciples of Bahá'u'lláh, Prophet founder of the Bahá'í Faith. Like so many heroes and martyrs before him, he arose to spread the message of this divine Revelation. He was sent as a pioneer to Burma. He reached Burma towards the latter half of the nineteenth century. He learnt the Burmese language and scriptures and worked tirelessly for his Faith. His son, Ismail was born in Burma. He was my grandfather. My mum was born in Rangoon.

I had several maids who looked after me. Sometimes we lived in our bungalow in the countryside. It had a big garden full of flowers that gave out a lovely fragrance. It was tended by two gardeners. The house was a large, wooden one, two storeys high. We also lived in an apartment in one of our multi-storey buildings in the city of Rangoon. One day, I saw the orphans of the neighbourhood march near our house carrying a banner in order to raise funds for the orphanage, People would throw them old stuff or money. I stood on the veranda and threw all my beautiful dresses down. My maid would complain to my mother.

"Look! Mona is throwing away her whole wardrobe. There will be nothing left."

"Leave her alone," my mother would remonstrate gently, "if that is her wish, then let it be. We'll get her some more tomorrow."

My uncle's wife, whom I called aunty, used to say that my mum spoiled me. I was her only daughter. I remember one night asking her for a skipping rope. She did her utmost in the very dead of night to find one for me.

There was an earthquake once. I was ill with a rash and admitted to hospital at that time. I remember being rushed through the earthquake in a car to escape from the city. Everyone was in a state of real panic.

My mother's legs were swollen. She used to cover herself with a sheet and say in a joking manner, "I am dead, I am dead!"

Perhaps she wanted to see my reaction. Perhaps it was just child's play. My father and mother used to argue. My mother would say, "It's my money. I can do what I like with it."

That would make my father sad because he had no wealth of his own and obviously no say in how she spent hers. She was always a big spender and liked to throw parties and give generously to the many friends who surrounded her. If someone admired a ring on her finger or a piece of furniture, she would immediately either hand it over to her or get a replica done.

I remember how much my father loved us. He would put us on his lap many an evening and feed us on the veranda of the house. My father had some problems with my maternal uncle. I heard them arguing one day. My father was not a good businessman. My uncle had given him money on several occasions to start a business. He was never successful. The business always went bankrupt. One day my uncle lost his patience. They quarrelled. My father went away and never returned. He went to Iran, the land of his birth and I never saw him again. My mother was very sad. She loved him very much. She was never the same again and her health slowly deteriorated. When she died I was only five years old I think. People said she died of a broken heart. I don't know if that's possible, but I think she was still very young–in her 30's perhaps.

I remember the three little birds. They used to perch themselves near her bed on the veranda. Then the little birds died one after the other. On the fourth day my mother too was dead.

She was well educated. I still have a picture of her holding a scroll. As a youth, she wore her hair in plaits but as she grew older, she wrapped it around a comb perched on top of her head, as many Burmese ladies did.

When she was ill, no one came to visit except her close friend Fatima. She was a poor girl who would sometimes run some errands for us. Fatima was her only true friend. She was there the day she died. After that I lived with my uncle's wife, whom I called Ama. She was part Burmese and had four children of her own but she looked upon my mother as her own child. When she married my uncle, my mother was still a schoolgirl. My 'aunty' bore children of her own much later in life.

My father wrote once from Iran. He asked my uncle to send his children over. My uncle refused. I never saw or heard from him after that. I think he re-married much later. My aunty took good care of me and my younger brother but life was never the same. I missed my mother very much. I remember Ama sharing all my beautiful clothes out amongst all the children.

I remember a little old Baha'i lady visiting us in Rangoon.

She anointed me on the forehead with some rose water. They called her Miss Martha Root. She was American and she did what no one ever did–travel the whole world several times over to spread the Word and financed herself by writing some articles in each country she visited. Queen Mary of Rumania declared her belief in the Baha'i Faith after granting Martha Root an audience. I recited these few words about living the life and she was ever so delighted,

"... to live the life is to be no cause of grief to anyone–to be as one soul in many bodies–never to allow oneself to speak unkind words about any other even though he be our enemy...If a man has ten bad qualities and one good one, look at the good one..."

She travelled with a small suitcase full of books, a few clothes and some curlers. Every time she arrived in a country she would kiss all the poor children that would crowd around her, some with running noses. I felt that she was very pure, kind and loving with no trace of prejudice of any sort–race, nationality, religion or colour.

I was about thirteen years of age when I contracted typhoid just before the war. I did not eat for many days. I heard them say that there was something wrong with my intestines. I ran a very high fever and the doctors had given up all hope of my recovery. My mother came to me in a dream that night. She came up very close and passed her hand so very gently and lovingly over my head! It was so real that I thought she had really come back to earth.

I screamed, "Mama, mama, wait for me! I am coming with you. Please don't leave me behind!"

She did not talk but with a slow and gentle wave of her hand she told me 'no'. I remember distinctly. She had a long white dress and her hair was long and flowing. I rushed towards her but she moved slowly backwards and I could not reach her, however hard I tried. I sobbed and stretched out my arms, but she slowly faded away. The next day, my fever had gone down and the doctor said that it was a miracle! I knew that it was my mother who saved me.

I was a teenager when the war broke out. I was still at the Convent school in Rangoon. They taught us how to lie flat on the ground at the slightest sound of machine gun fire. Burma was under British rule. The Japanese invaded Burma all of a sudden. The British were unprepared for war and most of them fled from Burma. Those that remained behind were very badly treated by the Japs and many were brutally tortured. I once caught a glimpse of some British prisoners. They were forced to work in the hot sun, stripped to the waist. A common punishment for those fair-skinned prisoners of war was to be tied to a pole and exposed to the cruel heat for long periods of time without any water. It was heart-rending to see the way they were tortured.

We lost everything in the war, and went from wealthy merchants to pauper. Our houses and buildings were bombed mercilessly and all the banks collapsed. We later sold the only bungalow we had left in the city to the Japanese in order to survive. When the British re-captured Burma, the money that we had left from the sale of the house had absolutely no value. Many a night we would huddle together in prayer, aware of the risk of being buried alive if one of the bombs fell too close to the shelter.

Another uncle, Mahmud, was very fair with brown hair. It nearly cost him his life when he was mistaken for an Englishman. He had to show them some pictures of his ancestors to convince them that he was of Persian descent. Uncle Mahmud Shirazi had built the Bahá'í centre in Rangoon and built up a small library. He was in love with his books for they contained the sacred Scriptures. The soldiers threw them all out of the cupboards and desecrated them. He was heartbroken. He used to live alone in the centre, writing books. He had one best friend, a Christian called Kassim. Not long after that, he died of a heart attack. Fortunately he was spared the sight of the centre lying in ruins after a night of merciless bombing. He never married. I heard that he was in love with a lovely Burmese girl. One day while crossing a river in a boat, she was raped by some men. She threw herself overboard and drowned.

Those who fought in the front lines and were the first to enter Burma were the Manchukos. They wreaked havoc in the country. Young boys were dragged and beaten. They were taken away from their families and forced to fight in the army. The girls were also dragged off and taken to the unknown. They were never seen again. When the Japanese army entered Burma however, all those who had ill-treated the local people were shot.

My cousin Hadi was also taken away by the Japanese and forced to fight for them. We gave him up for dead until he re-appeared after the war. He recounted many incidents. During the fighting he always managed to shoot into the air in order to avoid any human target. The Japanese used to kick some of their prisoners off a cliff. One day he was ordered to kick a British soldier off a cliff. He knew that if he refused he would be killed on the spot. He raised his head and prayed like never before.

Suddenly a fellow soldier standing beside him yelled,

"What are you doing? You are taking far too much time. Here, let me do it." The soldier reached out and the foul deed was accomplished.

Hadi returned from the war laden with gold and jewels. My aunty, poor as she was, refused to touch it. She would say,

"I don't want to have anything to do with this. They are stained with the blood of innocent men and women."

I don't know what my cousin did with the loot. I never saw a trace of it again and we were all as poor as before.

During the war the planes bombed the city till it was in ruins. Every home had a dug-out. When the sirens wailed, you could hear the screeching of the birds and the barking of the dogs. All nature seemed to cry out at the horror of war. We had to leave everything we were doing and rush to the shelters. Every night there was a black-out and we would huddle underground for hours. When the planes left, big trenches had to be dug to bury the dead. From the balcony of our house, I could see lorry loads of corpses, some with no head and some without hands. Some were still bedecked with jewels. There was no one to rob them. It was such an ordeal just to stay alive. The stench of death and rotting corpses filled our nostrils. Cholera and other diseases broke out and spread rapidly. People were scared to go out and get food. Shops were often closed.

A dear friend of ours who was also our private tutor and whom we called uncle, contracted cholera. My uncle, Abdul Husayn, was very brave. He stayed with him night and day despite the great risk to his own life. We used all the blankets in the house. He had to be washed and cleaned almost continuously. The house was under quarantine and no-one was allowed in or out except one person who brought us food. His last wish was to see all the children. We all went upstairs and stood around his bed. While uncle was praying, he died.

I recall another horrifying incident. A young girl was shot in the breast during the war. There were no medicines. Her brother had to squeeze the pus out every day. I don't know whether she survived or died a lingering death.

When I saw all these scenes of war, I became paralysed– stretched stiff with fear. My family did everything they could but I could not recover. They then decided to leave the city and retreat to a little village called Daidanaw, where I could be rubbed down with local herbs. Daidanaw was called 'Abdu'l-Baha's village because virtually all the 800 or so villagers were Bahá'ís. Mustafa Rumi had come to Burma from Iran in the latter half of the nineteenth century. He was a disciple of Bahá'u'lláh and consecrated his life to the spread of the Faith in that land. I remember the holy old man calling me every morning for a glass of water and we would talk for a while. He taught me a prayer in Persian or Arabic but I have forgotten it now. The people of that village were very kind and generous. They would greet any visitor very warmly and offer one anything they had! Even there however, we were not safe. It seems it was a time of intense nationalistic fervour and people of foreign backgrounds were in particular danger. I remember my cousin Ruhhiyih having a bath when all of a sudden we heard screams.

"They are coming, they are coming! Hurry up!"

Apparently in 1945, the village was attacked by a mob of 3,000 people who surrounded it to purge it from all foreign influence. The Bahá'í school and Bahá'í homes were burned to the ground and property looted. Some 11 Bahá'ís were killed in the attack.

A member of our family went up to Mustapha Rumi and urged him to flee for his life. He was 99 years of age. He refused to leave. The young man wanted to stay with him and offer him whatever protection he could. Mustapha Rumi, who was then very advanced in years, was adamant in his refusal and we had no choice but to leave him behind. Our hearts were heavy with grief for we knew what would befall him. When the wild villagers came they found him praying on his white rug in the Bahá'í centre. He asked them to grant him a last wish. He wanted to say a prayer before he died. As he knelt down and prayed fervently, they hacked him down and it is said that when they beheaded him not a single drop of blood fell on the spotless, white prayer rug. Perhaps that is what he prayed for. The people were so terrified that some fled from the spot shouting, 'Miracle! Miracle!' His body was hacked to pieces.

In the middle of the night, my uncle crept out under cover of darkness to recover his remains and give him a quick burial just outside the centre. He risked his own life in order to fulfil this dangerous task. Later on, this spot would be designated a foremost shrine in the community of Burmese believers.

The neighbouring villagers had somehow been incited by someone to rise against the Bahá'ís and they were intent on killing us. While we were fleeing someone threw an iron rod and it broke the arm of one of my relatives. He screamed day and night with the pain. There was nothing we could do as there were no doctors or medicine. He was never normal after that. His young son also lost his mind soon after that incident.

My only brother was lost in the jungle during the flight. He was around twelve or thirteen. He spent one night alone in the forest. We all gave him up for dead. I was heartbroken because we were very close, especially after my mum died. The next day however, he re-appeared, physically unhurt but traumatized by his horrifying experience. He described the sights and sounds of his nightmare journey through the jungle especially the sound of the bombs exploding in the distance.

"Boom! Boom!" he would shout, cowering in a corner with his hands pressed tightly over his ears. He lost his memory soon after that. All that he could vividly remember was that night he spent in the forest and the sounds of war. He had no recollection of anything else.

At one time we had given up all hope of survival. We all knelt down to pray as the villagers advanced on us, knives raised high in the air. My cousin jumped into the river but she was saved in the nick of time. Suddenly a man appeared and stopped them. I think it was a Japanese General. As we left, some people showed us a small hut where we could shelter for the night. We prayed a lot that night and while we slept someone crept in to warn us that it was all a trick. There was a plot to burn us alive that night. The man said that he had a bullock cart outside to take us to safety. He took us to a big house. It was a refuge. A Burmese family offered shelter to all who needed it during the war. That night we saw the little hut burning in the distance. After that a Buddhist priest offered us protection for a while. He told the villagers that what had been offered to him was sacred and could not be taken away. Eventually we thanked the family for all their hospitality and returned to Rangoon, a devastated city, to rebuild our lives or whatever was left of it.

We managed to open a small food shop and a Japanese officer gave us a piece of paper to stick on the door so that none of the others could hurt us. I was around eighteen years old when a couple we knew who lived in Rangoon asked my uncle if I could stay with them for a while. They had gone to live in a small village and were expecting a child. The delivery was very difficult and the pain the woman went through was agonizing. There were no doctors to attend to the delivery. The family members did whatever they could. The mother and her baby survived but she became mad. For a whole year she was a raving lunatic. She tried to strangle her husband and cut off all her beautiful hair. She never attacked me but I was taken back to my family in Rangoon for my own safety.

We were very poor. We lived in a very small flat in the ruined city and my elder cousin Ruhhiyih went out to work so that we could survive. Some days, we struggled to find food to eat! I lived with them until an old, wealthy Iranian friend of the family came from Pakistan to take us away. They called him uncle Baktiari as he had taken care of my father when he came from Iran.

Then one day the greatest tragedy of all struck. We were to be separated! There just wasn't any other choice. We cried all night long. We were devastated. The last night we spent together none of us could sleep. We were heartbroken. My brother clung to me like a drowning man to a straw. I thought deep in my young heart that even the slightest hope of his recovery was finally gone. I stayed for a while with a Bahá'í family while my brother stayed with Mr Baktiari who had a shop, a bakery and a restaurant. Uncle did his best to cure my brother. He brought many doctors and medicines but he could not regain his memory. He would disappear for days without telling anyone and then suddenly appear looking ill and underfed, his clothes in tatters. I was later taken to the 'New Era' Bahá'í school in the mountain resort of Panchghani where

I could help with the small children and in this way build a life of my own.

It was there that I finally met my future husband. I remembered the old beggar who came to our door after the war. We offered him food. He was so hungry that he could only eat a morsel or so. He called me and read my palm.

"Come here little one," he whispered, singling me out from the crowd, "You will cross the high seas".

That was all I could remember. The day I boarded the ship with my two children to join my husband who had pioneered to the remote Indian Ocean islands of Seychelles, the little old beggar's words echoed in my mind.

Little did I know that a whole new pioneering adventure was about to begin–with its manifold victories, joys, challenges and sorrows. We fought a different war there. We carried the trophies but also bore the scars of the great spiritual Crusade. Four more children were to be born under those bright, tropical skies

I lived with the sad memory of my only brother most of my life. We did not have the financial means to bring him over or to travel and meet him. I knew that if I could have been there at his side, I could have cured him but this was not to be. I shed silent tears many a night when everyone was asleep. One day, my husband and I finally had the opportunity to see him. Our ship had docked for a short while and uncle Baktiari brought him to the quay to see me before we set sail again. I was shocked by his appearance. He was younger than me but looked much, much older. His hair had turned completely grey but the saddest part of our encounter was his words of greeting when we were introduced.

"Munirih? Munirih is dead," he said. My sister is gone,

gone in the war. Boom! Boom! This is not her. I am tired. Let us go."

I tried to refresh his memory and assure him that I was still alive. It was to no avail. Too much time had elapsed and it was just too late. To re-open old wounds would perhaps cause more harm than good because I wouldn't be around to help him through all that confusion. The encounter caused me much more pain than it did him. In time I got to thinking that at least his innocence was his armour against the struggles of life. Death would free him from the shackles of his earthly existence. Not long after, we got news of his sudden death. Someone seemed to pierce my heart so deep that I choked and then turned stone cold for a moment. I had no more tears to shed. They had all dried up.

Suddenly a scene flashed in my mind. I was sitting alone on the steps of our apartment in Rangoon after the war when my brother suddenly appeared, carrying a piece of bread in his hand.

"Did Ama hit you? Are you sad? Here take this. I don't want it."

I knew he was hungry as he was still a growing teen-ager, so I shook my head and he sat with his head held close to me for a long time.

Suddenly I saw the rainbow after the rain. After all the pain, the shadows vanished one after another and the light filtered through the thick clouds at last. I knew then that he was happy. I did not have to worry any more. One day I know, we would be re-united as children again.

I outlived my husband. He was only fifty-nine when he suffered a major stroke after a short holiday on the idyllic island of La Digue. In medical terms it was diagnosed as a coronary thrombosis caused by the hardening of the arteries. He recovered slowly but never regained his full powers of speech or full mobility on his right side. He lived for ten more years and I was always by his side. It wasn't always easy. In fact they were some of the toughest years of my life, but I had learnt the art of patience and resignation over the years.

At the ripe old age of seventy, I still have the strength to look after myself and see my seven grandchildren grow up. I am still in contact with Ruhiyyih who migrated to Australia. I am looking forward to visiting her, this year. She is the only living relative I have managed to keep in contact with all these years. I met a Bahá'í youth last year who had been in Rangoon and actually met my cousin Hadi, who is now caretaker of the Bahá'í centre there. He sent me a picture of him when he went back.

Soon I shall be a great-grandmother with no ailments other than a failing knee and dysfunctional gallbladder with its chronic digestive problems. Life goes on… I only wish that when my time on earth is ended I go quickly and do not linger. I may not have drunk of the cup of suffering to the dregs but I have sipped of its crippling draught that shatters the illusions of youth. My earthly fate, inextricably woven with the threads of pain, ruin and loss and spun at the loom of sacrifice has been a tough struggle out of the vale of despondency on the steed of faith.

APRIL HOLIDAY

We watched them dance over the waters. They swoop towards the jagged reefs, and then soar sharply to touch with outstretched wings. They hover over the wind-tossed surf, madly flapping those snow-white wings to keep from dropping into the waves beneath. They dart in opposite directions, turning in concentric rings and race across the skies in complete abandon. Then they cross each other's path and clamber to a higher plane where they are joined by several of their own kind. The colours of several species mingle, as they cacophonously share the glorious sea harvest. They come to rest for hours in the branches of the giant casuarina, finding immense solace in the complete stillness and silent contemplation of each other's presence. In the trees one can distinguish the dark brown shapes of the Lesser Noddies. It is the start of the mating season and they perch in pairs beside the small clumps of algae that will serve as rather untidy nests. They click their long, scissor-sharp beaks, as they bow to each other in a quaint and rather comical gesture.

Along the beach, tucked beneath casuarina number seventy-eight, a mother incubates the egg. Its white tail streamers are a dead give-away as they protrude onto the beach. It sits very tight for it is acutely aware of the unfamiliar sounds all around. The head repeatedly turns in our direction, with the beak tightly shut. The black markings in front and behind the eyes, as well as the powerful yellow beak, give it a formidable look. A few moments later it struggles to sit up on legs far too short for the body and flies seawards into the sunset. The children are devastated. They discover the dirty-looking brown egg with tiny black spots and think that it has been abandoned forever.

"Oh no! Now she won't come back and the chick will never hatch. The geckos and skinks will eat it for sure."

The egg did look very vulnerable where it lay exposed to all the elements, but the brownish hue merged extremely well with the natural environment of sand and dry casuarina leaves. The next day we were quick to follow up on the incident. We were most relieved to find it back at its task. I watched it as it sat so engrossed and yet so relaxed, in the full bloom of motherhood. Its glossy crown glowed like white satin. The incubation period takes up to forty days. During that time, the mother has to leave the 'nest' to look for food. I wondered about its chances of survival. They were very slim from what I gathered.

Number seventy-six also had an occupant but it had not laid the egg yet. It faced landwards as the winds still blew from the north and it had no protecting tree cover. We eventually saw another Tropicbird under the casuarina tree close to chalet Golan. It did not stay long and we never saw it again. Perhaps the site was too close to the path for comfort and it left in search of a quieter place.

After lunch we wandered behind the pavilion for a few minutes of solitude. I was not alone. Under the Indian Mulberry trees, the undergrowth teems with wildlife, co-existing in perfect harmony and destroying only to survive. The giant Aldabra tortoise calmly selects its tasty morsel as it stretches towards the lowest branches of the *Bwa Torti* and then joins its mates cooling off in the pond. The three Magpie Robins hop along between the fallen coconuts, looking inquisitively at the intruder and making long, harsh, guttural sounds rather like air torn intermittently out of a balloon. One sharpens its beak after a delicious lunch of giant gecko. The trees are filled with myriad colours. The Seychelles Fody flits from branch to branch. The Lesser Noddies rest in pairs on virtually every branch in between the occasional Fairy Tern. One carries in its beak a dried leaf that it carefully wedges in the corner of a branch. The Brown Noddies prefer to nest in the coconut trees. The lizards are everywhere of course. As they rustle the dry leaves, one is always turning expectantly in the direction of the human intruder.

One very hot afternoon, we set out on a mini-expedition to the west coast to visit the unfinished cottage. This would accommodate visiting scientists and other guests. All the existing houses were occupied by the growing staff complement since the official opening of the island nature resort in 2000. The small cottage was perched above the red cliffs of eroded granite and the panorama was rugged and wild.

Privately owned for almost 200 years, the island changed hands frequently except for a more stable period between 1927 and 1945. We later discovered that a Jean Gontier bought the island in 1816 for some 1,300 lbs of cotton! With very few inhabitants at any one time, Cousine was exploited for Sooty Tern eggs and Shearwaters. Copra, tobacco, salted fish and brooms made of Guinea Grass were 'exported' to Mahé. Cattle were also kept and one can still see the marks left by the ropes on the coconut trees where the cows were tethered. Strange markings have also been seen on the rocks around the island. Too symmetrical to be weather features, some believe them to be pirates' legacy of hidden treasure.

On our return, we took a turning into the Pisonia forest–

home to thousands of Lesser Noddies. The coral-looking phosphate rock had been formed from guano deposits over the last six thousand years. It lay everywhere and the leaves and path were stained white with bird droppings.

I wondered how soon we would also be subject to the same treatment when Tyrian yelled, "Papa's got it all over his arm! Yuck!" No sooner did the words leave his mouth when his own foot suffered the same fate. I clutched my hat close to my head but emerged unscathed by a formidable stroke of luck.

A few coconut palms along the way were a sure sign that we were close to the sea. Out in the ocean, a huge granite boulder sculptured by the waves into the shape of a benign old man, gazed towards Silhouette and North Island. It sent a friendly warning to poachers. We named him *'Bonhomme'* because of his flowing beard of brown algae and his big round rose.

We tread very carefully on our return for the path is crawling with giant millipedes and several varieties of lizards. The Wright skinks are slow and heavy and cannot scurry away as fast as the Seychelles variety. As we look around, we are astonished by the number of baby Fairy Terns of various shapes and sizes. They were perched on rocks and branches in most precarious-looking positions. Their well-developed, webbed feet however allow them a very firm grip and thus prevent them from toppling over. The mothers fly very low over our heads, quite unperturbed by the intrusion. Then we suddenly stand transfixed by a sight so delightful to behold! High up on a branch a mother feeds its young chick. It swoops down with a sizeable silver fish in its beak. The chick needs no urging. It reaches down and grabs the helpless creature head first, swallowing it in two deft movements. Only a fraction of the tail is visible from where we stand. The delicious meal however feels more of an ordeal than a treat. The young chick struggles valiantly for several minutes. Its tail moves up and down as it tries hard to force the meal down its digestive passage. I had read that Fairy Terns do not regurgitate the food for their young. Instinctively, they choose the right size of fish for the chick. Peter the warden, however, had witnessed the fate of a baby Tropicbird that stayed close to his house. It had suffocated on a meal that was too gigantic for its size. We were therefore very apprehensive as we watched the whole operation. The mother sat close by. When it was satisfied that all was well and the chick was past danger point, it flew to the next tree. It was careful not to disturb the baby. Its eyes were closing with exhaustion after all the strenuous exertion. The mother meanwhile, preened and cleaned its feathers after all the assaults at sea.

Further along, another female lands on the wrong branch. She listens attentively. I can hear a chick cry. She flits to another branch and carefully shuffles along it. It was then that I spot the small brown ball of fluff. The mother holds the fish horizontally in her mouth. The chick must not loosen its hold on the branch as a strong gust of wind could dislodge it. The mother's sharp beak must not hurt it either. She holds her position, moving her head closer. The chick pecks at the fish. The mother turns her heads sideways but the chick is not satisfied with mere morsels. It pecks hard and removes the fish from the mother's beak. It is a precarious situation. The fish is held sideways and the chick cannot swallow it whole so the mother reaches out and grabs hold of it in her beak. A split second later, the chick grabs it back. This time it is held correctly, tail first and swallowed whole. The mother slowly shuffles over to her and from behind envelops her with her breast to warm and comfort her or see her safely through the digestive process. Ten full minutes elapse before there is some movement underneath. The mother prods it with her beak as if to say, 'What's up?' and then closes her eyes in tiredness. On high alert, she opens them at the slightest sound or movement. In close embrace, mother and child enjoy these few rare moments of intimacy on a few centimetres of branch. Who knows if they will ever share such warmth again!

On the way back we spot a beautiful baby Tropicbird at the foot of a tree, nestling in a rock crevasse. It was a sheer ball of white fluff. Its wings were streaked with black, rather like silken lace on an expensive white satin, party dress. They often betray their presence by screeching when people pass by. At the slightest sign of an imaginary threat, it rises ably to its defence with sharp and vicious attacks of its beak. Its whole body stiffens in a very aggressive manner. It emits raucous sounds to frighten everyone away. The short, webbed feet, rather like a duck's, are clearly visible as it rises to strike back.

Even this idyllic life is not without its disappointments. The last of the season's batch of Hawksbill turtle eggs had hatched the day before. Peter, who had been keeping a careful watch, had discovered myriad tracks running down the beach that afternoon. We were nowhere to be found so he called the children to witness the last moments of this wonderful yet poignant event. They had taken some thirty-eight hours to emerge. Twenty-seven had been eaten by crabs. Twenty-five weaker ones were salvaged while a couple had not been fertilized. The remainder had most probably made their way safely to the sea since they were nowhere to be found. I first caught sight of them as the fiery glow of sunset faded in the sky. The small blue bucket that Peter brought down to the beach was teeming with tiny brownish black bodies, desperately moving their flippers about. We put them all gently down and watched in a mixture of joy and sadness as they made their desperate bid for survival. They crawled in all directions moving their flippers awkwardly, like a baby learning to crawl. The flippers seemed too long for their tiny bodies and a few turned over and lay there helplessly stuck in the wet sand. Some had a few minor deformities. One flipper would not straighten out, however hard we tried. Perhaps it had lain at the bottom of the batch and the compression of the eggs from the top had affected it. Their shells had already hardened and this would afford them some protection at sea. A few were entangled in the seaweed and could not break free. Some returned to shore with the next wave and had to be promptly sent back. A few kept going sideways and we wondered if they would ever make it to their destination. Without human help, I guess some twenty-five percent would perish in those first few moments of orientation, as they run their first great marathon to the life-giving ocean. The children were overjoyed each time they rescued one of these vulnerable creatures, so overwhelmed by the hazards of their environment. I guess that was why nature had the mother lay so many eggs at one time. I wondered if they fared any better at sea. Peter had once accompanied them a hundred and fifty metres from the shore. They swam non-stop all the way, as though putting as much space between them and the threatening shore. Then all of a sudden they stopped swimming and just bobbed about like a cork on the waves. No fish or shark bothered them yet.

I watched the last of those tiny black dots pinned to the

crest of the waves and swept into the vast unknown. They slowly faded into the night. There was nothing more we could do except bid them the very best of luck.

Years later, during the turtle season in December, when we were helping ecologists Frankie and Dylan walk the beach every hour, a record of five came up to lay one morning at the North end. By December 14th, thirty-one hawksbills had already laid. We were told that their productive life may start at thirty years old. They lay around three times each season and live for over a hundred years although no one knows the exact average life span. The hatching period lasts some fifty-four days but one has to check after fifty days.

My first sighting of a hawksbill coming up to lay was an overwhelming experience! I stood stock-still as I came face to face with one of the rarest phenomenon of modern civilization. This wild creature crawling out of the surf somehow lands on an untamed shore to give birth in the probable cradle of its own birth.   Awkward and apprehensive, it moves very cautiously, all senses on full alert. From a distance it could easily be mistaken for a rock or piece of coral covered with algae. Then it moves! Knowing that its range of vision is quite limited I move very slowly and position myself behind it. Like all sea creatures, the dazzling hues of a shell that shimmers in the filtering light of the deep blue ocean, quickly loses its brown and yellow gleam in the harsh sunlight and turns a dull, greyish brown slate. A special species of barnacle that moves like a torpedo has managed to fasten itself to the carapace.

It seems to pull itself up the beach on its back flippers first, hence the higher piles of sand at the lower end. In the centre of the tracks, the cloaca leaves a faint mark in the moist sand, unlike the prominent gash of the post-natal journey. A highly armoured reptile, the hard shell gives way to a tough orangey-yellow casing that extends beneath the body. Its head, a mosaic of grey and black, contrasts with the yellowish pink of the extremities and a neck that reminds me of an accordion, with folds of skin that can be pulled in or out in response to the external environment. The two tiny nostrils are hardly discernible above a mouth shaped like a hawk. It raises its head often as it appears to scan the landscape and sniff the changes in the surroundings. You discover just how wild the hawksbill really is when you try to pat its head on its way down. It recoils from your touch as though from a bad sting and moves faster than ever out of your path. Just how strong and flexible its flippers are, I was soon to find out.

This one rested at the upper part of the beach, just below the high water mark. I saw one climb a seven-foot sand dune in the mid-day sun, to lay amongst the creepers. They can come up in the hottest part of the day because they can regulate their body temperatures better than the larger Green Turtle. This particular specimen averaged forty centimetres in curved length and as it turned I noticed that the edge of its shell had been broken or chipped off either by a shark attack or some jagged piece of coral. Dale, the beauty therapist, had seen one with a missing flipper that laid a record of over two hundred eggs that season.

The turtle started to make its body rest. Both sets of flippers spread out the sand and then it starts to dig the nest, scattering sand some two metres away, even up to my face. I knelt, mesmerized by the spectacle of such dexterity, precision and perfectionism in so heavy and clumsy looking a creature! The edges of the flippers start to look like a two-dimensional human hand with stunted fingers and a claw. The hind flipper picks up the sand like an ice-cream scoop and flicks it forcefully away, then presses on the edge of the hole to make it firmer while the other flipper flicks the loose sand from the outer edge of the hole. Like a potter at her wheel, this continues for over half an hour until a round hole emerges shaped rather like a light bulb. Peering down, I could see the round markings left by the flipper as it scooped the sand out in a circular motion. The nest is now elbow length and the turtle's back is tilted almost twenty-five degrees but it still continues. By now I am joined by Frankie the ecologist, the Cosmopolitan editor and a couple of Swiss tourists. Frankie's husband Dylan passed by and laughed.

"You look like people at a wake; all peering down at the coffin."

"Well, yeah," I acknowledged"–celebrating the miracle of birth in the contemplation of the certainty of death."

"It's about to lay now!"

Frankie tensed up as the flippers suddenly stopped flicking sand and the body stiffened as the muscles started to contract forcing the first eggs out. They are on high alert. Usually, if the turtle lays below the high water mark on in a crab infested area, the nest has to be dug up and the eggs transferred to a safer place preferably before seven or eight hours have passed. If not, they have to be placed in the same orientation otherwise the movement interferes with their development. To economize on the time and energy spent in digging up the eggs, they slipped a plastic bucket covered with sand directly beneath the turtle. Soon hundred and forty-four eggs lay moist and gleaming in the blue bucket. Soft enough to cushion the impact of the fall, yet crusty enough to protect the embryo, they look like ping-pong balls but weigh some ninety grams.

When the last eggs were laid, the mother remained in the same spot for a while and kept pushing the sand back into the egg chamber with the hind flippers until it was all covered up. Then it slowly moved forward, scattering the sand with its front flippers. Dark eyes and eyelids were smeared with sand.

"What's she up to now", I asked, wondering why she was not done with her herculean labours.

"Camouflage!" Frankie explained. "She's trying to disguise the spot where she lay."

As she spoke, Frankie dived down quickly and stuck a twig deep into the sand to demarcate the egg chamber. Just how important this move was, I was to realize in a few minutes when it had shuffled some fifteen feet of sand and I could not for the life of me identify the exact location of the nest. Frankie came back later with a pair of metal rods. She pushed them deep in the sand, in a criss-cross position. The meeting point identified the exact place to dig. A number tag showed how many had laid that season while a number painted on a coconut impaled on a spike showed the beach zone. Suddenly the turtle turned and made its way to the sea, stopping many times and lifting its head to gasp for air and smell the scent of the ocean while checking for signs of danger. Once in the sea it looks as light as a cork but does not swim very far. I could see the head come bobbing up for air but it stayed a short distance from the North shore. Maybe that was its permanent home as snorkelers often spot one around the big rock.

On my last night, turtle, number SEY 42824283, laid a hundred and two eggs over a period of two and a half hours– from six to eight-thirty pm. It had already laid in October and was in fact the first to lay that season. It seemed quite old for it was 76 cms wide and 85cms long. Strangely enough, when it had dug three-quarters of the way, it inexplicably ambled away from the hole and shuffled around the long grass and creepers at the top of the beach for some ten minutes. Having finally decided to dig another nest in the same terrain, it tore at the roots of the plants, seemingly effortlessly. Frankie and I were talking in whispers when it suddenly stopped digging and without even spreading its flippers the usual way, started to lay the first batch of eggs.

Hey, I think she's started!" she exclaimed disbelievingly. "She must be desperate!"

We were caught unawares but Frankie was quick to react. She reached into the hole to pick up the eggs and count them quickly before cupping her palm beneath the back of the turtle to catch and count the eggs as they fell with each contraction.

We watched, Frankie and I, with a warm intensity that matched the soft Asian blue of an evening sky that exploded into a bright crimson ball that dispersed a huge mushroom cloud over the western horizon. I saw the first bright light of planet Venus come up in a sky soon to be lit up by so many stars that it looked like a depiction of that holy night in Bethlehem on Christmas day. The moon rose later and the only sounds were the flapping of wings and the squawking of the Noddies that intermingled with the pounding surf close by. I could feel my body merge with the ebb and flow of the tide and soft sea spray that oozed into every nerve and sinew bathed in moonlight and starlight. The soul, rejuvenated in the bosom of the earth, expanded into universal space framed only by the boundaries of the imagination. Lulled by its rhythmic echoes, it beats in harmony with the reality beyond the shadows of night.

The next day we set off for the west side cottage, built on

the overhanging cliffs of rusty red, eroded granite that afforded a spectacular view of the ocean. The path to the hill started behind the electricity generators and Peter's immaculate work shed. This was to be the residence of the environmental staff and visiting scientists. With the opening of the hotel resort in 2000, all air-conditioned houses already built would be occupied by the staff and management. This included the beach chalet next to the pavilion, with its reed-covered roof shaped like a kraal.

In 1971, a German bought it through 'Polar Star Company Ltd' and built the Mediterranean-styled villas amidst the huge granite boulders on a hill top. Many casuarinas had by then been introduced on the beachfront. The island was finally sold to a South African businessman who decided to turn it into a nature reserve. Part of the environmental costs would be met from four deluxe villas that allow tourists an intimate encounter with nature.

One hot morning we set out for the north end and the cave that lay at the bottom of the cliffs. The place was covered with *Pisonia* trees. They provide some eighty percent of cover on the island. The path was flanked by *Mange Tout*, a small green plant that is not endemic to Cousine. It was a delightful walk. A trained eye could detect baby Fairy Terns on the edge of the rocks and the branches of the Screwpines. A very young chick, all fluffy brown and white, sat tight on a rock. The brown markings had a greyish tinge. The older ones were of a lighter brown. The colour fast disappears to make way for the snowy-white down that earned them their ethereal name. They always looked so mournful with their heads pulled in, and their beautiful coal-black eyes staring straight at you. They shy away from all human touch and are best left alone. On an overhanging branch, a small egg lay precariously close to the edge. It merged well with the colours of the tree for it had brown dots and purple patches against a white background. It was carefully laid in a small groove on the branch. Apparently, the geckos sometimes knock them over and then rush down for the feast. A strong wind could also dislodge them.

We clamber over the huge granite boulders and find the large and impressive entrance to the cave. It is accessible only at low tide. To our right, a Tropicbird drops almost vertically into the sea from a great height rather like a fighter-bomber plunging to its doom. It was a sensational dive. The cushion of air cells under the skin in front absorbs the shock of the diving impact.

The high entrance of the cave had an intricately ornate, reddish-brown facade of pink granite. It had sculptured, green and white flower designs that intertwined beautifully with the complex patterns in the rock. A strong musty smell penetrated our nostrils. We gazed at the long fine thread-like algae that hung down from the roof like cobwebs in a spooky house. The little pool at the entrance was temporary home to some tiny fish and a baby moray eel that was quick to camouflage under a rock. The floor of the cave sloped gently uphill and was strewn with mother-of-pearl. Fragments of polished granite lay everywhere and they shone like dull gold. Further inside, the light faded slowly away and the cave widened before it narrowed at the end. We had to stoop to enter. It is around two metres at its widest, as high as thirteen feet in places and as long as thirty metres. At the end of the cave, a pile of soft clay and boulders lay on the floor. It was testimony to the fact that wave erosion was a current phenomenon and the cave still under formation. We did not tarry any longer. The tide was coming in and the water swooshed round our feet as we reached the entrance and made a hasty exit.

Every morning and noon we make our way to the pavilion, a spread of sheer white elegance along the shore. She is built in old French colonial style, with white, latticed frames, through which the Seychelles Foddies weave in and out in a quaint ritual. The white, high-pitched roof which glitters like silver in the bright sunlight is adorned with the traditional, symmetrical, dormer roofs. The facia boards have a lambrequin trimming in the shape of a man in a hat. A beautifully designed balustrade runs all along the edge of the wide restaurant and open lounge. Occasionally, a Tropicbird, attracted by the bright sea blue cushions, rests comfortably in the armchair. The bar with its octagonal roof, that resembles a lemon squeezer supporting a queenly crown, is situated at the Northern end. It overlooks the polished granite walls of the flower beds that are filled with white periwinkle. The pool terrace of flamed granite is decked with elegant, white, garden chairs. At the opposite end is the spacious library, filled with books for nature lovers. On a nearby cabinet, an old dhow with bright, orange and red mainsails is a reminder of the nineteenth century Arab trade routes and the days of the early settlement. Several Roman-styled divans rest against the walls, beside the bright, blue and white vases and low, coffee tables. The deep blue cushions contrast with the dark brown wood of the furniture. A large writing desk offers a welcome facility for those who wish to research in peace and seclusion, unless of course, you are compelled to play 'Cludo' for hours on end with a pair who is set on winning each game. A beautiful sunset hangs against the wall like an erupting volcano in sensational colours. It contrasts with the pale watercolours of a more peaceful afternoon by the sea.

One morning, we were lucky to see a pair of dolphins frolicking quite close to shore. They somersaulted back and forth in an amazing display of skill that lasted several hours. Then they disappeared for days.

We had just finished lunch and were enjoying our cup of coffee in the lounge, when Peter was seen scurrying along the edge of the pool with a long pole in his hand. He plunged it into the pool and held something very tenderly in his hand. From a distance we could distinguish the tail of a very wet skink that had suffered a terrible mishap. All Peter's efforts appeared to be in vain. The lizard remained motionless.

"Give it the kiss of life," we shouted light-heartedly.

We then froze. Peter actually responded by putting his head very close to the skink's. Moments later, he deposited it gently on the side of the boat. He insisted that the CPR had revived it. We secretly thought that the amount of air he blew in would most likely explode its tiny lungs. That was quite the greatest feat of conservation we had ever witnessed!

My son was more fanciful. " It might turn into a princess now," he mumbled thoughtfully.

"Oh yeah!" Peter agreed, straight-faced. "To-night, on my way home, I'll no doubt bump into her under the trees. I'll have to marry her at once.''

The pavilion is ethereal at night. Dimly illuminated, it lies against the dark silhouette of the mountain ridge, under a starry sky that is a sure sign of another scorching April afternoon. The lights are subdued and the soft strains of music soothe the senses. The lone moor hen swims undisturbed in the unoccupied pool until Fred, the owner, spots it and bundles it off into exile on Mahé.

"This moorhen has the biggest toilet on earth," Rieul commented, watching its antics."

Then the clouds to the east are laced with fiery silver and orange. A full moon emerges from behind the horizon, like a great orange ball rising in slow motion behind the giant casuarinas. It rises later every night. Once we were surprised by what looked like a gigantic star or planet suspended above the ocean. Surely, we thought, Jupiter could not have gravitated so close to earth! It turned out to be only the light on the mast of a yacht that had cast anchor just outside the island. The lights in the cabin cast an eerie glow over the waters, rather like smugglers stealthily waiting to cast their loot ashore.

Peter of course, could only anticipate the horror.

"A rat can easily swim ashore from that distance, "he declared vociferously. "I might just decide to climb onto a pair of jet skis, haul a giant fin over my back and circle their boat all night. That would frighten them off! When are those skis arriving Pete?"

"Oh, very soon–perhaps next week. I have a picture in a magazine if you're interested."

As Pete, the manager, shuffled off to his office to show us a picture of his future acquisition, I had visions of Cousine's veteran 007 careering round on the latest jet skis, in order to preserve the pristine environment!

We love to retire after dinner in our large comfortable chalet, built in the same French colonial style as the pavilion. The natural, rustic green surroundings are a sharp contrast to the comfort and luxury that lures you inside. The rear patio faces the mountainside and the huge granite boulders are home to thousands of sea birds that fly to and fro all day long. A

Noddy once collided with the facade in front during my nocturnal meditation. That shook me up a bit. The sparkling white walls of the chalet are broken by a strip of Blue Pearl granite that runs along the middle. The Roman-styled divans and carved teak furniture add a distinct touch of classical. From the central cabinet, music and television is accessible from several channels but the natural sounds of the birds and the waves transport you to a world where sounds blend in perfect harmony. In the middle of the spacious chalet, the King-sized bed is fitted with a white mosquito net that falls gently from a wooden supporting frame. It is tied back by the identical, bright, blue and yellow material of the soft furnishings. Full blown photographs of beach scenes and the pavilion in the last glow of the setting sun, fill the walls. The fishes feed beneath the reefs and a baby tern looks timidly on, as you pass by. The kitchen has all the amenities you could desire on a holiday—even an ice-maker! The front and rear patios offer completely different but equally breathtaking views of the island. They are the world's best nature observatories, all furnished with armchairs, granite tables and chairs. The movable deck chairs beckon you to the grassy lawn outside. There you can feel the gentle touch of the wind on your skin as it combs through your long, dark hair.

Aride Island is visible from the front patio. To the left, the island of grey granite boulders close to the shore is a recommended snorkelling spot. Although the reefs are not as spectacular as they were before the abnormal rise in sea temperatures, the underwater world is filled with colours and sounds that beckon you further and further into their depths. Parrot fish in dazzling green, blue, purple, red and brown shades swarm all around. They are heard before seen. As they bite the coral, the staccato sounds of hundreds of mini-explosions fill your ears. The more sombre-looking zebra fish have black and silver-grey stripes that earned them the name of Sergeant Major. They nibble at the reefs and even at your back–but they are no cause for alarm. The birds whizz by overhead with small fishes or algae in their beaks. You sometimes wonder if they feel like a touch of your wet hair as nesting material. They can feed way past sunset and you wonder how good their eyesight must be. In front of the pavilion and quite close to shore, swarms of mackerel circle around you in an unbroken stream of silver and white.

One hot afternoon, armed with metal rods used to demarcate the turtles' nests, we went octopus fishing with Berard on the reefs at low tide. Born on Silhouette, his real name was Joseph but his parents and friends preferred to call him by his middle name, Berard–after the priest who baptized him–in the hope that he would emulate the good Father. Apart from fishing, his skills included the drying of copra and the weaving of traditional, bamboo fish traps. He explained how he mastered the art.

"Started learning as a child but first they gave me the stems of coconut leaves 'cos they are easy to bend. To-day, I can make a trap in two days…if I concentrate!" What he really meant was that a drinking spell may interfere for days with his work programme.

Story telling was his other art…Selwyn and the boys had gone bottom fishing one day and the fish would not bite. Tyrian was very disappointed so Berard tried to distract him.

"Hey, the same thing happened to me and my friends a while back. We fished and fished and caught nothing. Suddenly, my friend felt something big and heavy at the end of his line. 'Help me pull', he cried. We pulled and pulled until it finally came up. Guess what? It was an old black pot with its lid on and d' you know what? It was still steaming. When we opened it, we found a *la daube banane* in it."

He kept a straight face throughout and I think they almost believed him.

One day, a young shark forced its way into Berard's fish trap. Several coral fish including the tasty cordonnier were devoured by the predator that also broke the trap in several places. Berard was furious. He went shark fishing off the rocks by the headland the very next day and almost every other day after that. He caught a small shark. He suspended it on a tree by his house. The other workers asked him what this was all about.

"It ate my fish alive so it will suffer the same fate–no mercy he'll get from me–oh no!"

Seven years, he worked on D'arros island. It was owned by an Iranian prince. One event stuck out in his memory.

"This guy Oreddy was walking on the beach one day. Suddenly he found an arm cut off at the elbow. It looked like a white man. Who knows? Perhaps the crew of a passing ship had a fight and an arm was chopped off. Maybe a stowaway was thrown overboard. One day I went to look for lobsters in the reef at low tide. There, entangled in the seaweed was a whole skull! I also saw some bones–maybe of the arms and legs. It was the remains of a skeleton. We buried it anyway–gave it some sort of burial."

He was so casual about these things that I almost had some misgivings about the truth of the matter!

"Once a fishing boat from Desroches capsized close to D'arros. One drowned but one was saved. He went from island to island at low tide but couldn't find anyone. We were all on the main island at that time. On the island called Ressource, he stuck his shirt on top of a giant Casuarina. We thought it was just someone from the Russian vessel. Then David Albert from Praslin brought the Iranian prince's family to visit the island. He saw someone run across the jagged coral reefs to meet him. He looked like a wild animal. They fed him and took him to D'arros where he was flown back to Mahé."

Berard used to dive for lobsters on Mahé in some fifteen feet of water using just a mask and flippers. Of course he encountered sharks, ..."these pointy-faced ones with a white under belly," he called them. "Look them straight in the eye and they shy away but then they can slide up behind you so you've got to keep turning to face them." He was more scared of the barracuda.

"Always dive in pairs! They change colour when about to attack. Like chameleons, I've seen them change to the colour of sand and then seaweed. Then they start to sway from side to side. Hey, better get out fast man. They can come up very fast from behind so you've got to face them too. At St. Joseph, we used to catch lobsters in the reef at low tide especially before the arrival of the royal family. Some nights we could fill three bags full–as many as sixty lobsters! We would enter the reef at high tide, beach the boat and wait for the turn of the tide to hunt lobsters. At the next high tide we would leave the island."

His experiences on Silhouette were very different.

"There was an old guy–Kapolo he was called. He must have been almost a hundred years old when he died. The wake went on for three days. No one wanted to bury him so finally the police was notified. By then his body was all dry and shrivelled up in the coffin. When the people saw the police coming, they ran with the coffin to the cemetery. There was just no time to dig the hole so they dumped the body in the Dauban mausoleum, and ran up to a recent graveside, pretending to be covering the tomb. Satisfied, the police went away."

Of course they removed the body later but Berard was elated by the idea of a poor black man sharing in death, the tomb of the rich and renowned family of French descent who owned and ruled over the island for so many years.

"Kabulka lived at Anse Mondon. He was a sort of witch doctor. Saturday nights, after moutia and drinks, he announced that he was going to Mauritius to get some more drinks. He went to the beach, took a bamboo basket that was used to clean rice and swivelled it around with his fingers. Then he sat on it. We saw him disappear over the horizon. Two hours later, we heard someone blow the conch and when we ran to the beach, we found him there with a crate of wine. He said it was still warm. People would buy the drinks from him while women would order cloth. People thought that he killed fat kids and put them in his magic pot. One day, a father told his fat son that his life was in danger so they spied on Kabulka when he went in the bushes. The day he went to Mauritius, they passed his excrement all over the door of his house. When he returned, he was furious. He scraped all the shit and put it in a kettle to boil. Then he marched off to complain to the island administrator. On his way, he suddenly developed stomach cramps. He began foaming at the mouth and a few minutes later he dropped dead. From that day onwards, people say that a fat kid managed to outwit the sorcerer!"

Berard was quiet that afternoon. It was very hot and being low tide, the reefs were half exposed. We prodded and poked in every nook and cranny.

"Just look out for holes in the coral or sandy patches," Berard counselled. "The octopus eats out a hole in the coral with its mouth and rests in it after feeding beyond the reef at high tide."

He made it sound so easy but after one hour of scouting around in the scorching sun, we headed back to the beach pretty disappointed. Berard had been so sure of his prey.

"Come quick! Come! I found it!" Berard yelled all of a sudden.

We sprinted back excitedly and peered and peered at a tiny crevasse in the coral. I couldn't see a thing!

"There! Can't you see a glimmer?" He pointed at a tiny piece of coral at the entrance of the hole and pushed it aside.

"Look! There is the tip of a tentacle. Come on! Poke it until it comes out. Here! Take my rod. It's sharper."

I still couldn't see a thing but I poked into the tiny aperture and was amazed at how deep it went.

"Harder! Harder," Berard urged." You have to hurt it otherwise it just won't come out."

He handed the rod to Tyrian to try but he didn't succeed either. It seemed to move further in with each disturbance. Watching the men on the reefs on Mahé, I always thought that a simple prod would taunt it out of its hide-out. Berard poked viciously a few times but then he was forced to reach deep into the hole and try to wrench the creature from safety. Few seconds later something shot out of Berard's grip like a missile in awesome attack. Then, like a beautiful and deadly flower, it opened out in the shallow green water amidst the brown seaweed and white coral, its translucent ivory skin streaked with light brown providing an incredible camouflage. Berard dived for it again and the myriad tentacles, each some fifteen inches long, immediately curled around his forearm. It was a young octopus but the powerful suckers would not let go and the skin was pulled almost an inch from the flesh as each was plucked off using all his strength. The shiny, slimy, slippery body slipped from Berard's hand and as it hit the water, the last of its defence mechanisms was activated. Four times it ejected a dark, inky-coloured liquid that turned the sparkling, aquamarine pool in which we were standing, a muddy brown. For a moment we completely lost sight of it but as the colour dissipated, Berard's experienced eye detected it a few feet away, desperately hugging a large piece of coral. He plucked it up and as he held it high in the air, the large piece of coral came up with it as the powerful suckers clung on tenaciously.

"Look! Just see how strong the bugger is. It can carry all this weight effortlessly."

Then Berard dealt the death blow. He tore at a thick flap of skin in front until it detached and then turned it inside out. The octopus stopped struggling after a few twitches as the brain ceased to control the body. Holding it by the head, he handed it to me.

"Here! You can take it back to Mahé and make a nice meal."

I thanked him. I usually love octopus salad but my appetite for it seemed to have suddenly vanished. I thought I would feel elated after this successful hunt. We had robbed the sea of one of its elusive, natural phenomena. It had fought so hard for so long, using all of nature's wiles that I was left with an overwhelming and inexplicable feeling of guilt and loss.

Later that evening, I sat at the writing desk beside the carved, antique-looking mirror and gazed into the ocean, I daydreamed and tried to draw some inspiration from the streamlined shapes of many colours that fluttered in and out my mind. At the back of the chalet, I spot our very own baby Fairy Tern perched on a branch close by and surrounded by Lesser Noddies. It was not more than a month old. It never moved except once–only a few inches–to shelter against a fork in the branch. Sometimes it slept with one eye open. I never saw it being fed. Once however I saw an adult close by. It may have been the mother. I really hoped it was.

The bathroom has a great, white Jacuzzi for those who prefer a more tumultuous time in the bath. A starfish and a pink, golden-tipped, abalone shell, hangs in ivory and blue frames against the white walls. A small, bright blue, butterfly vase sits on a shelf of Blue Pearl, in gleaming white surroundings.

One afternoon, we bade good-bye to the staff that actually looked sad to see us go. Sheila was her usual perky self, until Pete's bulging eyeballs reminded her to forego her rustic ways and serve the meal from the correct side. Chantale wore her warm and genuine smile. Cecile stood nervously by as she tried her very best to do everything right. Didier, the sous-chef, was looking forward to a week off. He had worked extra hard since the departure of the chef a month before. I hoped that they would all still be there when we visited again. Rough seas had to be navigated as efficiently as the calmer waters. The ocean of life is visited by many seasons.

After that, we reluctantly made our way to the small, grass clearing next to the beach, fringed by clumps of white periwinkle. The sand dune, visible from where we stand, slopes into a stagnant pool of water trapped by the slope of the beach and replenished at high tide. It is home to a solitary stingray and some other small fish. The only marks visible on that beach are the tiny feet of the Turnstones that look like four-leaf clovers. They leave a distinct set of tracks as they search for their prey lurking under the stones on the beach. I remember coming across a young Fairy Tern learning to fly further along that beach. As I approached, it took off rather precipitously and clung awkwardly against the trunk of a casuarina. Its wings were outspread. Fortunately it did not stay in that uncomfortable position for very long, but flew wisely down to the roof of the boat shed. I had seen one pinned to a tree trunk like a rag doll. It had been less fortunate and was never able to extricate itself. What a tragic end to a flying debut!

The sound of the main rotor of the gleaming white and red helicopter fills the air. The grass and flowers are flattened to the ground. It drops effortlessly onto the landing pad. Everyone rushes to unload the precious cargo and equip the passengers for the return journey. The pilots keep to very tight schedule. They offer an extremely professional and efficient service. They are Cousine's most reliable means of transport, for she does not have a jetty. During the south-east monsoons, landing can be a tricky affair. The price to pay for conservation can be a heavy one.

The helicopter lifts off in a heavy burst of sound but the peace and tranquillity is locked within. It is a heightened consciousness of new dimensions–a harmony of chords as ancient as the rich black earth on which we tread or the soft white feathers that fill our horizon. Nature has virtually no frontiers on a granitic island that is as natural as it gets. This was no mere holiday. You are never a mere observer on Cousine. You are a contributor to the preservation of a global heritage and an active agent in the fulfilment of a philosophy that has already left imprints on the pages of natural history. The immense respect and care for every harmless, living thing that the island culture inculcates, breeds a sharpened awareness of a microcosmic universe at one with itself.

I realised then, that this would probably be the last time we visited the island before the paying guests arrived. I hope that while revelling in the natural treasures, they leave behind only footprints in the sand and a lasting love that will preserve our unique heritage from the trials and tests of time.

NORTH

One cloudy Sunday morning, we reached the deserted bungalow in Bel-Ombre. Its glass doors were wide open. Pepé discotheque was close by. We turned towards the beach and parked beside the white Buckie. Müller was unloading basic supplies for the island. He was bare-chested, heavily sunburned and wearing the skimpiest of bathing shorts. That was North Island's project manager. Eighteen years of Government service and the management breed somehow brought to mind a distinct species of bureaucrat.

The boat that was anchored some distance from the shore finally came in. It was a 25 foot catamaran with 100 Hp; twin Yamaha engines, all imported from South Africa. The trip took about an hour. A catamaran is usually a steady boat in calm seas but during the south east monsoon, it's a veritable rock and roll across the waters. The boat sometimes veered dangerously but the boat boy kept speeding nevertheless, confident that he could keep the boat on course.

As we approached North Island via Anse Cimitiére and rounded the headland–a rocky outcrop with a giant cross–I could sense the tension in the air.

"It's very dangerous out here," the boat boy announced by way of assurance.

No one answered. No one moved.

"The waves are quite big. It's tough going."

He suddenly revved the motor and sped in front of the onrushing waves. We turned around and sure enough a big wave was racing us. We made it in the nick of time for we were very close to the rocks. The pass through the reefs is very narrow. The boat was still tossing wildly when we helped moor it to the buoy or 'corps mort' as they call it. He reversed towards the beach where it was anchored more securely by the island staff that were splashing waist-high in water.

As we waded onto the beach, I scanned the shore excitedly. How much could have possibly changed in just a few years? It was virtually a deserted island then. Some old, dilapidated workers huts, a derelict manager's house, the ruins of a *kalorifer*, an old store and boat house were the only relics of a once flourishing past. From pirate's cove to artist's haven, it became market garden for some eighty inhabitants who fished, farmed and even exported some fine quality products locally. Crops thrived on one of the most fertile soils in the archipelago. A young South African and his son were the only inhabitants. He was employed by the new owners, 'Wilderness Safaris', as a sort of caretaker. They lived in the old boathouse and slept in a hammock. Their drinking water was from a bucket in a well. One thing stood out in my mind. His son was afraid of the dark. The cure was administered promptly—exile to a tiny, triangular, telecommunications shed on an exposed hilltop, with only a torch and knife for survival

The beachfront looked exactly the same. Even the empty carapace of an old tortoise, bleached white by the sun, lay in the identical spot under the Takamaka tree. The old table and hard wooden benches of the thatched boathouse had merely changed place. Several electric bulbs however hung in strategic places and a brand new radio and cassette player seemed the focal point of entertainment for the Zulu workforce who passed by unobtrusively. The rickety petrol stove had disappeared and a hose pipe lay on a rustic, concrete sink at the back. The derelict, manager's house, once the administrative hub of the island, was in exactly the same condition, right down to the cracked window panes and chipped coral foundation. The old storehouse, built some sixty years back, with its cracked floor and walls of coral mix, sported a new corrugated iron roof and industrial burners. It had been turned into a spacious staff kitchen. It had a long central table, a giant freezer and little else; at least for the time being. Its arched doorway looked out on the most beautiful scene in the world; an ocean of glittering shades of sapphire that sent crashing waves on golden sands and fresh, salt-laden gusts that rustled the overhanging leaves. The old coconut kiln with its rusty metal shelves had been put to good use. The outer end of the giant drum was now the island oven. It baked unique island bread, product of the sheer ingenuity of a cook driven to wits end by the scarcity of produce as opposed to the huge stacks of flour in the corner of the store. Dijon's lumpy but tasty bread was served morning, noon and night. After a few hours it left an incredible pit in your stomach that made you feel quite faint and craving for more!

Beer was the first person to greet us. He was responsible for the first phase of the construction project. This involved the staff quarters and the basic infrastructure. The second and final phase would be the ten deluxe villas by the beach, a swimming pool by the rocks and a gym and spa on the hillside. It wasn't Beer's first job in the Seychelles. He had worked on a thatching project on Frégate Island Resort and even had enough time to acquire a girlfriend on Mahé. Attie followed, notebook in hand, trying to look as formal as possible in just a skimpy pair of shorts–the best way to economize on underground water and labour by cutting down on the washing.

"Hi! Welcome to North. Great to have you. I'll show you to your quarters Your bags are already there. Lunch is at mid-day."

I looked down as we walked. My feet were black and covered with a fine dust. The path, once covered with grass and shrubs was denuded of vegetation as the giant Caterpillars rolled back and forth. North, like Silhouette, is one of the younger islands of the Seychelles group. It is only some sixty-five million years old as compared to the seven hundred million of Mahé. The magma solidified quickly, cooling under the sea at the same time as the Indian sub-continent was being formed and the dinosaurs disappeared. The granite had more quartz and was rather whitish in colour. The colour of the soil was probably due to the top soil enriched by humus from the cattle and guano deposits of a bygone era.

"How are the tortoises doing?" Selwyn asked by way of conversation.

"Great! They're all there."

The owners had bought twenty tortoises from Mahé for thirty-six thousand Rupees. That was a first step in the eco-tourism project that aimed to restore the island's natural eco-system. Rats would be eradicated and endemic plants and birds re-introduced as part of a Noah's Ark vision. Trees such as the Lantern Tree, Cabbage Tree and the Portia Oil Nut would provide nesting places and attract the sea birds while the Paradise Flycatcher, Magpie Robin and White Eye would be brought in as protected species. At the moment however all the birds I could see were a couple of pigeons.

North has a wide coastal plain and the coconut trees were among the tallest I'd ever seen. Slim and straight, they seemed to reach for the sky. Attie must have read my thoughts.

"Oh, we inspect them regularly One day a tree fell just in front of me. Hey, it was so close, the leaves brushed my face. I cut one the other day over thirty metres high."

"Did you hear of an incident involving an ex-Miss South Africa?" Selwyn laughed. "She was employed by 'Wilderness Safaris' on a conservation project and pitched her tent outside the boat shed. Every night, she would jump up in fright thinking that elephants were on a stampede. She just couldn't get used to the coconuts falling!"

"Reminds me of the film 'Castaways', I added. Every time a coconut fell, he got ready for battle against an invading army."

We saw some of the workers dehusking coconuts for a cooling drink.

"My way's far simpler. I just drive the Caterpillar over them."

Attie had obviously not mastered the local art of bashing them on a vertical wooden spike driven into the ground and sharpened at one end–not quite as simple as it looks! Takes quite a bit of practice not to impale your hand instead!

Flanking the path were the old workers huts still resting on their wooden stilts. The walls of coconut timber, the thatched roof and wooden floors and shutters were all of local material. These tiny, dilapidated huts, hardly more than fifteen feet long must have been claustrophobic if not for the draught from the wooden flooring. Those that had undergone recent maintenance rested on limestone pillars and had corrugated iron roofs. This time however, there were unmistakable signs of tenancy– clothes on the wash line or suspended from the open windows. Something new then caught my eye. Close by was a weird kind of windmill. Beside some makeshift screens and close to a tree were a few large containers each with a chimney and a whirly-bird that revolved madly in the wind. These were the famous enviro-loos used so successfully in Australia because they dispensed with water. The chimneys extracted the air using wind and heat to dissipate the stench. Judging from the whiffs that came our way, the humid, tropical weather of the Seychelles was surely putting their environmental friendliness to some severe tests.

"Well! Here we are. This is the architect's house–got to leave you now but see you later by the beach."

Tucked away in the recesses of the island was a veritable little colony. It was amazing! Twenty workers chalets accommodated some thirty-two staff. They were all of assembled pine, in single or double units. There was a large common area. The open dining room and office quarters were virtually completed but the laundry and store were still under construction. Grass re-planting had begun in earnest and some young shrubs carefully tended. A Frangipani tree outside our chalet had put out her first bloom.

"How long are they gone for?" I enquired.

"Two weeks I think. They're due back mid-September."

A big tent stood outside our chalet, the one that seemed furthest away. As we climbed the wooden steps, crossed the small, bare veranda with its exercise bike and entered the bedrooms, I took in the scene at a glance. We did not know what to expect. I was so glad to be able to visit the island again. The couple had a baby–that was obvious. Toys were neatly stacked under the bed and a car seat lay on a chair in a corner. With some relief I took stock of a ceiling fan, electric bulbs, a shower and of course the now familiar enviro-loo. At least we had electricity and running water. That was already more than I had hoped for. Even a mosquito net lay on a bed in the corner. A thick film of dust lay everywhere. I immediately wiped it off with a wet rag but it quickly returned. I had to forage for pillows. They seemed a scarce commodity on the island. We were very relieved to find a few lumpy ones.

We settled in quickly and made our way to the boathouse for lunch. There, on some hard wooden benches facing the sea, we met Dijon and tasted for the first but certainly not the last time, his popular island bread–product of his creative genius. Lunch consisted of beef stew and rice. Just how local the beef really was, we were to discover in due course.

After lunch, Attie invited us to visit his chalet. I held my breath as we walked up the pine steps leading to the veranda. I just couldn't believe that this was an identical unit to ours, except smaller. It was transformed into a veritable work of art– a hide-out of remarkable taste. The plain steps were lined with segments of coconut trunk from which fresh, green fronds brushed our calves as we passed by. The light that filtered in through the pine shutters had a warm, soft, cosy sort of glow. A corridor had been contrived from hanging mats of coconut leaves, braided by an Indonesian worker from Bali. It led from the veranda to the bedroom. The same curtain material was used to create an alcove that became a walk-in wardrobe and tool cupboard. A mirror on the wall was tastefully framed with dried bits of timber bleached by the sun into myriad shades of brown and grey. The pine bed had become a four poster centrepiece. Old bits of gnarled timber and driftwood salvaged on the island were adorned with narrow strips of coconut mats. Old bits of coconut tree trunks served as lampshades. An ancient takamaka plank, probably part of a floorboard had become a small bench in the corner of the room. Rustic shelves of varying shades of timber were fixed to the wall and joined with sets of thin, pale bamboo rods sharpened at both ends. They formed a shape rather like a harp. Years later, I would remember this beautiful miniature as I walked around a deluxe resort that used the same art forms but in a far more spectacular way.

"Here are my shells", Attie proudly announced as we peeped into the alcove. "I spend my evenings sorting them out into small, medium and large–that–and of course the interior décor."

On the wall I noticed something somehow incongruous with this island setting. It was a large poster depicting African wildlife. Next to it was a bow and set of arrows.

"This looks pretty professional–any use to you here?" I asked.

"I'm a professional hunter."

"How does one become one? Are there formal courses?" I had never heard of a degree or diploma in hunting.

"Oh yeah! I followed a two-week course but the practical component lasts six months. D' you want to try?"

He brought the bow down and tried explaining to the boys about Bear bows and compound bows. His was a fifty-five lb Recurve bow without sighting because of the survival aspect. You had to use your naked eye to become a better natural hunter. The only contact the boys had had with bows and arrows had been birthday toys.

"I shot my first game when I was six, using a Triple 2 calibre rifle. It was an impala. At seven I put down a wart hog and at eight a Kudu."

"But of what use is it here?"

"Cows!" he pronounced with a gleam in his eyes. "I go after the cows."

"Co...ws?" I stuttered disbelievingly.

"We want to restore the island's natural wildlife. This means the extermination of introduced species such as cows."

"How many are there?"

"Oh, quite a small herd–five males including the old bull and four calves. They're not as easy to hunt as you may think. Initially I could catch them easily but now they can sense my approach. I have to use my bow and arrows–get them right in the chest– puncturing the lungs–quick way to go. It's even getting worse. They now run when they see me so I got to be extremely cautious, creeping stealthily in the long grass–using all my hunting skills."

"Can we try them?" the boys asked.

"Sure."

Attie took down the bow and started to string it. That itself didn't look at all easy, for the bow, that was heavier than me, had to be bent first. Then we all took turns.

"Posture is vital. Keep your back very straight or you could injure yourself."

The boys could only move the arrow back an inch or so. I managed only a couple more, using all the strength I could muster.

"My God! No wonder in the films Robin Hood stands so erect."

One had to keep the back very straight and take a deep breath before taking aim. If you didn't it could be the weapon of your own destruction. I thought of my first horse ride on La Digue. It looked so easy in the cowboy films. Trotting was easy enough but try galloping and you end up shaken up and clinging ignominiously to all parts of the animal just to keep yourself from crashing to the ground. You wonder how people could ride for miles and look like they were enjoying it!

The next morning we saw one of the ill-fated cows. It was not grazing in the open field but strung up by the neck with a giant hook nailed to a branch in an open air abattoir next to the old Takamaka tree. A contraption made of fine netting kept the flies away from the exposed flesh. Attie had obviously had a successful hunting expedition. By mid-morning, it had been gutted and skinned. The guts, skin and bones lay splattered on the ground. It had to be carved, filleted and carted to the kitchen where all the fillets and loins would remain suspended from the ceiling until its final journey to the mincer. Everything was minced. The meat was so tough. We were to partake of this delicious minced beef throughout our stay—in stews, meat balls and curries.

Early afternoon, I spotted another cow in the 'abattoir'. Attie had made a grand kill of two that day. The next day, on our way back from Grand Anse, I came across the herd of cows—or what was left of it. They were grazing in one of the brightest green pastures I had ever seen. It was the dried up marsh that was now filled with what looked like papyrus from a distance. As we walked by, the herd gazed up at us with great mournful eyes, looking as tame as cows could be. I was to learn later however, that in time they became so wild and dangerous that even Attie was no match for them and the army had to be called in for the final extermination.

The journey to Grand-Anse was a very pleasant one as it was shady most of the way. The path was lined with all kinds of fruit trees—sour sop, guava, breadfruit and orange. *Takamaka, Calys du Pap* and *Badamier* trees were very prolific. The beach on the other side however was very exposed and the reefs lay very close to the shore–certainly no ideal bathing place except at the far end where a cave had been carved in the cliffs some distance from the beach. Some of the reefs reared almost six feet high. One tall piece of coral branched out like a human skeleton as the waves battered it over the years. As we strolled to the southern part, the island of Silhouette was clearly visible. I wondered about the exact spot of the shipwreck over two hundred years ago, and how much or how little, must have changed over time. They first tried to land on Silhouette after fifty days at sea, subjected to the cruellest extremes of hunger and thirst.

According to archival reports, a Portuguese captain, Anacleto Gomez, set sail from a town in the state of Tamil Nadu, on the 20th September 1783, in order to reach a major port on the east coast of Sri Lanka. Terrible storms ripped the sails and the ship drifted for some three to four months. Many perished from hunger and thirst. One lascar threw himself into the sea out of sheer desperation while another hanged himself. They survived on seawater, urine and dried fish. The first sign of hope came in the shape of the Fairy Tern. They tried to anchor but the anchor cable was cut by the coral. In the morning they sighted an island. It was Silhouette but they couldn't land. They then turned to the neighbouring one and anchored in five to six fathoms of water at eight pm. on the historic night of January 24th.

The people on board would have seen numerous turtles going up on the beach in the moonlight to lay their eggs. They were so close to paradise, yet had no way of getting there until two crew members decided to swim ashore and build a raft during the night. The sea was so rough that during the night, the anchor cable was again cut by the coral and the ship tossed about wildly until the morning when she hit the jagged reefs that ripped her apart instantly. Fortunately everyone managed to scramble ashore. Some even managed to rescue their personal effects although badly damaged by the sea. As the desperate band of survivors combed the island, they must have come across the marsh where I had seen the cows. It was full of land tortoises, soaking in the stagnant ponds of brackish water. They fed on the tortoises and birds for a whole month until they got fed up of the diet and the dirty water. They looked longingly out to sea, wondering if they were to spend the rest of their lives marooned on the island. Some larger islands in the distance beckoned them. These could be inhabited. Finally, a vote was cast and they started to construct a raft or *câti-marron* from bits of timber salvaged from the wreck. The only tool was a blunt knife. When it was finished, five people got on board and were immediately half submerged in water as the so called raft could barely float. They had no food or water with them and were equipped with a bad sail and three planks that would have to serve as paddles. They spent a whole day and most of that night at sea. By sheer luck they reached the tip of St. Anne island. The waves overturned their raft but threw them inside the reefs so that they could swim ashore without great difficulty. They had actually reached the first settlement in the Seychelles–the St Hangard Establishment. After resting, they were transported to Mahé. The administrator of the islands immediately despatched two *pirogues* to the rescue and brought the rest of their companions to Mahé.

I realized that we would never know the exact spot on North where the first known person–a Portuguese sailor–set foot, but that it was on that stretch of beach, we could be certain.

That afternoon, we climbed the cliffs by the boat shed on which the giant cross stood. At the top was a small hut made entirely of coconut leaves. A small hose pipe brought water all the way up. The view and the tranquillity were out of this world. This was Attie's first home away from home. It was to be the site of the hotel spa and gym while the swimming pool would be just below, nestling between the rocks

On our last night, Attie invited us for a barbecue at his place. He had built a sort of open kraal with slabs of coconut tree placed in a circle. He called it a *lapa*, the Zulu word for people sitting around a fire. In the intimacy of firelight and smoke filled air, we discovered that his real name was Adrian but his parents insisted on calling him by his dead brother's name.

"Since I've come to the island they call me Mcgiver–'cos I can fix anything. I grew up on a game farm in Free State, close to Bloemhof dam. I helped with everything on the farm. On North I do the same. I'm a problem solver–a Jack of all trades."

"But how did you manage to find work in the Seychelles?"

"Hah! That's a long story."

His parents broke up when he was still young. He went to nine boarding schools and changed practically the same number of jobs. The fitter-turner turned soldier, trainee-pilot, thatcher, farmer, refrigeration technician and welder finally realized that he wanted to see the world and helping someone market slate art overseas was his ticket out. But the beautiful Tania, Beer's sister was the key.

"One day, I went to Neisner for a visit. I was very shy. I came across this beautiful girl on the road. Too shy to approach, I followed her to her car and slipped a note on her windscreen with my name and address. By sheer coincidence, she walked into the coffee shop where I was sitting with my dad. I walked out and put another note on her car telling her where I was sitting. Imagine my excitement, when I saw her walk back in! She wanted me to meet her mum and her brother. She wanted him to approve of me."

I did not ask about the fate of his relationship with a girl who needed the approval of her brother first!

"We're still good friends though. I worked in the thatching business for a short while with her brother. Years later, I was in Parys to meet someone who knew about a company in Johannesburg that helped sponsor the marketing of slate art overseas. I saw Beer drive past. I got him to stop to say 'hi' when he told me that he had a contract on North island. Did I want to come? Did I? Hey, Seychelles was like a dream paradise for me. I almost screamed in delight. What an opportunity!"

"How do like it now?"

He sighed contentedly. "It has been the best time of my life. I can create here. The challenge is to cope with what every new day brings."

He went up to stroke the fire. We did not see him again before our departure. The next time, it was at Sam's pizzeria in Victoria many years later. I did not recognize him at first. His long blond hair was cropped short and he had married a young Seychelloise. He had left North and the last I heard, he was working on another island.

Dijon had prepared succulent barbecued chicken marinated in fresh lime, served with jacket potatoes and green salad. One of his eyes had grown very red. We thought it was conjunctivitis but he believed it was due to stress.

"I've been working a whole month without any leave. I don't know what Mahé's like. I came straight from the airport to North by boat. Cooking here isn't like cooking on a well-stocked luxury yatch in the Mediterranean and Red sea or in Cape Town for extra dollars or just for socializing. Improvising can be a real headache when stocks are low. I've also had some bad news. My wife's car was stolen recently. That leaves her really in the lurch with the baby."

Dijon had been in the 32nd battalion–a platoon leader in the Caprivi region–a strip of land lying between Botswana, Angola and South Africa. They were a multi-skilled, specialized force composed mainly of mercenaries from Australia and Belgium. Only twenty out of five hundred were South African.

"What were they doing there?"

"Training Angolan refugees to fight the UNITA rebels backed by Cuba. I was shot twice. The first time was during the Moscow-Vietnam operation to take over Quito–a terrorist stronghold. I was shot by a sniper in the right thigh and lost consciousness. The next thing I remembered was a doctor pushing his finger in the wound to remove the bullet. The next time I was hit by grenade shrapnel during patrol inside Angola. We had to get information for the artillery from our observation posts. D'you know where that was? A tree! I spent three days up a tree on reconnaissance duty. I remember running out of food. We each had fourteen twenty-four hour ration packs to last two weeks. There was bully beef, baked beans, fourteen litres of water, chewing gum and water purification tablets. You couldn't wash with soap or brush your teeth in case the smell gave you away. When I ran out of food, I survived by catching fish in the delta or eating snake."

"Cooked or raw?"

"Raw. You couldn't make a fire–too dangerous. If you dared to take that risk, you had to dig deep in the ground or cook in your helmet. I weighed under fifty-four kilos–really skinny guy–but the army really drilled endurance and discipline into me."

"Any good memories at all?"

"Oh yeah! Getting a parcel of goodies from home and …finishing the army. Not having a girlfriend was a special bonus."

"Why?"

"Friends of mine shot themselves when their girlfriends ditched them."

After the army, he worked as boiler maker since he was specialized in stainless steel welding. From a kibbutz in Israel, a yatch in the Mediterranean, an oil rig off the coast of West Africa and selling melons to tourists in Mykonos, he ended up as barman in a pub in the UK. Finally, he decided to return to his homeland, working as boiler maker in Mossel Bay. From his savings, he bought a small apartment in Blu Strand, Cape Town. He surfed during the day, made pizzas for sale at night and partied all night long until he turned thirty-one.

"I got a loan and set up my own engineering business like my old man. I met a nineteen year old, long-legged blonde. My first son, Darron was born but I was rarely at home. I had contracts up country. The marriage lasted eight years. We divorced three years ago. I met and got married to Lisa a year ago–had to sell the firm to pay off my ex-wife. I then bought a small construction firm–loved to speculate in old houses since my youth. I started in Cape Town, and then moved to Neisner."

"Hence the Beer connection."

"I had a contract to do maintenance on some old buildings

on the waterfront. Just five weeks ago, I was busy painting someone's roof when James's brother's ex-wife Tracy called me.

"Hi!" she said. "Don't you want to work in the Seychelles?"

James was the sub-contractor for the construction of the workers' chalets on North. I literally flew down the ladder.

"Speak to me!" I yelled.

"There's no position in the construction and engineering field but can you cook?"

"Well, yes. I enjoy entertaining."

It was 3.30 pm. on a Wednesday. I had to fly to Seychelles that Friday morning."

"That was a hell of a rush!"

"Hey–no joke. I had one day to close my firm, put everything in storage, send my wife to her mother's in Johannesburg. That Saturday morning I was on the Johannesburg flight to the Seychelles, leaving my wife and baby behind."

We left North the next morning by boat. Dijon came with us. We dropped him at the Victoria hospital so he could get his eyes examined. Amazingly enough, it seemed to get better by the minute as we headed out to sea. He seemed to read my thoughts.

"See! Now they'll think I was just kidding or rubbed salt into it so I could get off the island. I think it was just the stress."

"You do need a break though. Perhaps the news that they may have a job for your wife on the island was the best salve possible."

We said good-bye at the hospital. It was the last we would see of him. On our next visit to North a few years later, he had gone.

This time we arrived by helicopter. The helipad was at Petite Anse so gone were the casuarinas and the little knoll and telecommunications shed where the frightened kid had been exiled. A club car driven by our personal villa attendant, raced to greet us. The very charming guest relations personnel also accompanied us to the central pavilion. The landscape was familiar–tall, slim coconut trees and grassy lawns dotted with old workers huts, once more uninhabited. The trees however were being skilfully scaled by a Seychellois labourer to eliminate the fear of falling coconuts. His colourful bonnet tucked in the long Rastafarian dreadlocks.

We wandered round the sprawling, open, central area and felt very relaxed in the rustic looking, quiet pavilion with its high Indonesian styled roof of Alang-alang, Rosewood floors and Teak furniture. Waterfalls cascaded into rock pools and bamboo bridges at the rear end while great curtains of five million seashells hung from the ceiling All along the beachfront, upturned trunks of uprooted Takamaka trees buried in the ground formed gnarled pillars that supported the whole superstructure, their thick roots weaving their serpentine way along the edge of the roof. A sense of opulence in the heart of untamed, semi-arid Africa overwhelmed me as I strolled towards the bar where the boys were already pivoting round on smooth, rounded, tapering, casuarina logs that served as bar stools. The great beams of dark Leadwood contrasted with the open deck of sandblasted pine, through which the granite rocks of the beachfront protruded and the light coloured tables and chairs merged into the golden sands outside. The old Takamaka tree was still there, providing extra shade for the deck chairs and sun shades placed close by. The carapace was not in its usual place by the old tree and as we left the reception area, we found that the giant Takamaka tree on which the ill-fated cows had been strung had been reduced to a stump just outside the new kitchen. Gone also were the rusty shelves and drum of the old coconut kiln in which bread was baked for the island staff. The area was now occupied by the toilets of the dive centre. The old kitchen and storehouse were now the library and dive centre office. All of the outer walls were retained but cleaned up and repaired, using materials from the existing island buildings, to give the whole complex an air of antiquity. What remained of the coconut mill was propped up outside, close to the old bleached carapace that had somehow survived the great upheaval. The old manager's house however, had not and there was no trace of its existence.

Our villa was a phenomenon–a feat of art unparalleled in Seychelles tourism. A long wooden bridge with thick wooden railings led to a four-module villa built on concrete pillars. Coconut trees, casuarinas and others grew from the floorboards. Upturned casuarina trunks became decorative pillars, alongside the main ones of Indonesian Bamuas and their roots intertwined with the concrete of the roof. The kitchen walls were of old island materials salvaged during the demolition works while the rest of the modular complex had the high traditional Indonesian roof of Alang-alang supported by gum poles. Everything was that unique mixture of rustic sophistication. The sandstone of the bathtub felt Medieval and the toilet had quaint wooden shelves, and bamboo curtains. From the bathtub you could see the shrubs and lawn outside. A plunge pool beckoned in the middle of the open deck that ran all along the front. Huge couches lay beneath a convex roof supported by natural tree trunks across which filmy white curtains oozed an air of imperial grandeur.

Jumping on our bicycles and equipped with light surfboards, we rode off across the mountain to the East coast for some surfing. The landscape seemed virtually untouched except for the newly built concrete road that ran all along to the end the beach where the cave was. We were not alone. A very friendly barman was permanently at your service at Sunset bar, a thatched shed furnished with logs and cushions and an old boat. The waves were not ideal for surfing so we settled for a swim instead and then headed back for a work-out. Attie's little hide-out was now a gym. with large glass windows through which one could see the shoal of mackerel and the gusts of wind dart across the deep blue ocean in dark patches. The beautifully maintained pool perched on the mountainside did not contain seawater as originally planned but overlooked the whole beachfront and central pavilion.

That night, Rob, the island manager gave us a PowerPoint presentation on the hotel construction. An amazing 50,000 tons of material was barged in and unloaded manually onto dumpers using human chains. True to the Noah's Ark concept, thousands of endemic trees and shrubs had been re-planted and thousands more growing in the nursery. The greatest challenge they faced however was the eradication of rats which they hoped to achieve by the repeated dropping of rat pellets by helicopter.

The return to Mahé was by boat and the sea was rough. Some of the workers were taking their leave. We were all completely drenched. There were no raincoats and the towels that we cringed under afforded only limited protection from the crest of the swells that whipped over the sides intermittently. We disembarked at the new port and I rode home at the back of a pick-up. The wind tore at my face and blouse as we raced across a highway that transformed the scenery and pastime of the inhabitants of the east coast.

As we journeyed home, past and present wove tapestries of nostalgic beauty that merged in shapes and forms that seem to stretch far into the recesses of time. Fantasy, taking flight from the vale of mediocrity and practicality and defying the impositions of tropical weather and budgetary limitations, could at least carry you on the wings of aesthetic revelry even for a short, enchanting moment in time.

ABOUT THE AUTHOR

 Born in 1956 in Victoria, Seychelles, the author has lived most of her life in the Seychelles except for four years in the UK pursuing her University studies and almost 3 years as a UN Volunteer in the Kingdom of Bhutan. She has an Honours degree in English, a PGCE and an MBA. She has often travelled abroad on holiday, short courses and official duty. She was employed by the government of Seychelles for 16 years, in the various fields of education, employment, public administration, human resource planning and development and gender issues. She was Seychelles consultant for the drafting of the first Commonwealth HRDP. Her last post was Director-General in the Ministry of economic planning, from which she resigned in 1999.

In 1999, she was appointed Auxiliary Board Member by the Continental Board of Counsellors for Africa for Propagation of the Bahá'í Faith in Seychelles. She served till 2012, during which time she also published a history of the Faith in the Seychelles, entitled, *'The seeds are sown'*. She is married, with 2 sons and has been writing poetry since her teenage years.